TAROT
CARDS

TAROT CARDS

JANE LYLE

Originally published (in a slightly different format) under the title *Tarot*, in 1990
by Hamlyn an imprint of Reed Consumer Books Ltd

This edition published in 1994 by
L & P
Michelin House
81 Fulham Road
London SW3 6RB
and Auckland, Melbourne, Singapore and Toronto

ISBN 1 85152 685 4

Produced by Mandarin Offset
Printed and bound in Hong Kong

A note on your Tarot deck:
The cards included with this book are based on the
Marseille deck, a classic Italo-French design which
remains one of the most popular worldwide. We have
illustrated the book with both the Marseille deck and
the Waite-Rider deck.

CONTENTS

◆◆◆

WHAT IS TAROT?

*Once condemned as 'the rungs of a ladder leading to the depths
of hell', Tarot cards have fascinated people for centuries. Prized by
gypsies and magicians, linked with witchcraft, and denounced as
heretical by medieval churchmen, Tarot has survived every twist
and turn of fortune. Today, decks are widely available – while
Tarot enjoys an unprecedented popularity.*

◆ ◆ ◆

The standard modern Tarot deck consists of 78 cards. These are divided into two sections; the Minor Arcana, which means 'Lesser Secrets', consisting of 56 cards, and the remaining 22 cards which are known as the Major Arcana – meaning 'Greater Secrets'. It is the latter cards which have variously intrigued, enraged and puzzled scholars, moralists, and a mixed bag of other seekers after the truth – including mystics, psychologists and occultists.

THE LESSER SECRETS

The Minor Arcana contains its own mysteries. At first glance it clearly resembles the deck of playing cards most people are familiar with. It is divided into four suits: Wands – also known as Staves or Batons; Pentacles – also known as Coins or Discs; Swords, and Cups. Each suit consists of numbered cards, from Ace to ten, and four court cards.

These suits are easily linked with suits of an ordinary deck: Wands correspond to Clubs; Pentacles to Diamonds; Hearts to Cups and Spades to Swords. Indeed, the name 'playing' cards may have been coined to clarify the difference between these cards and the ever-mysterious Major Arcana. In modern Italy they still play a card game called *tarocchi* with the Minor Arcana.

The actual symbols representing each of the minor suits also appear elsewhere in myths and legends. In Ireland, the legendary 'people of the goddess Dana' (Tuatha De Danann) spoke of four magical treasures: a cauldron, spear, stone and sword. Similar symbols are found in Hindu art: the cup, sceptre, ring and sword. Perhaps the most thought-provoking link is with the Greek goddess of Fate herself, Nemesis, whose symbols included a cup, a wand of apple-wood, a wheel and a sword.

Such symbols are also linked with the

four elements of the ancient world; fire, earth, air and water. In turn, these form one of the foundations of Western astrology, which groups the twelve signs of the Zodiac into four larger groups – each governed by its element.

THE GREATER SECRETS

The Major Arcana remains elusive for it does not obviously correspond to anything we can recognize today. Like the enigmatic statues on Easter Island, the inexplicable existence of stone circles, or sightings of ape men in the Himalayas, these 22 cards have spawned an imaginative range of theories regarding their origins.

Ancient Egypt is a popular background for speculation; some stories connect the cards with the writings of Hermes Trismegistus, legendary mystic, sage and supposed author of *The Emerald Tablet*, and other magical manuscripts. Gypsies, a word believed to derive from Egyptians, are thought by some sources to have carried the Tarot cards with them from India during their travels.

Other stories claim that when the great library at Alexandria was destroyed, the ancient city of Fez became a centre for mystics and philosophers who travelled there from the four corners of the earth. These wise men had a little trouble communicating with one another, since they all spoke different languages. So, the story goes, they created a symbolic pictorial language of their own which was designed to encapsulate universal knowledge and spiritual truth.

Some historical facts

Colourful speculation aside, the idea that the Major Arcana is a book of esoteric teaching is probably not far from the truth. The reason for this conclusion is based on what is known of Tarot's history.

What seem to be the earliest existing Tarot cards, of which 17 remain, date from 1392. Thirty years later, an Italian artist called Bonifacio Bembo painted the only full deck which survives from those times. These were commissioned by the Duke of Milan, and are known as the Visconti deck – after his family name.

So, if Tarot cards did exist prior to the 1300s there is slender evidence to support such a theory. But that is not to suggest that the ideas and beliefs behind Tarot's powerful images are as recent as the cards themselves.

Certainly, a number of images found in the Major Arcana seem to be essentially medieval, drawing on key figures and concepts of the time. The Pope, the Magician or Juggler, the Fool and the Day of Judgment would all have been familiar concepts – very much everyday features of the medieval world and mind – and seem to suggest that Tarot is a purely medieval invention.

But what about the surreal landscape shown on the Moon? And how can we explain the presence of a High Priestess, a concept which is still anathema to some Christians, or the topsy-turvy figure of the Hanged Man who remains serenely alive? These images point to a much older system of beliefs, for they have their roots in pre-Christian times.

Picture this

Medieval Europe was a dangerous place for heretics. By recording secret philosophies and teachings visually, those who disagreed with prevailing doctrines may have thought they had found a safe way to pass on their knowledge without incurring persecution.

The Renaissance practice of using what are called *ars memorativa*, that is pictorial memory systems, was an integral part of the whole occult movement at that time. This idea, intended as a meditation aid, was adopted from Ancient Greece; examples are found on talismans and amulets of the period.

Tarot could easily have been a highly-sophisticated pictorial memory system, and is still used as a focus for contemplation today.

THE INFLUENCE OF THE GOLDEN DAWN

Astrology, gnosticism, ritual magic and the complex Hebrew Kabala have all been linked with the Tarot, and have influenced its interpretation. Many of these correspondences were devised or refined during the great occult revival that took place in the nineteenth and early twentieth centuries.

The Golden Dawn, a short-lived but powerful magic order, was particularly notable in this respect. Arthur Edward Waite's book, The Pictorial Key to the Tarot was published in 1910. Another member of the Golden Dawn, artist Pamela Colman Smith, designed a deck of cards under his direction; this deck remains very popular, and is pleasant and helpful to use.

Another former member, self-styled Great Beast and controversial magician Aleister Crowley, also published a guide to the Tarot. The disquieting but beautiful images were illustrated, to his specifications, by Lady Frieda Harris – a talented painter. These images were first available as actual cards in 1969, 22 years after Crowley's death. They are known as the Thoth Tarot after the name of his book – The Book of Thoth.

PSYCHOLOGY AND THE TAROT

Much modern Tarot interpretation is influenced by popular psychology in general, and by Jungian psychology in particular. Carl Gustav Jung, (1875–1961) originally a pupil of Sigmund Freud, broke away from Freud's system of psychoanalysis to establish a richly-symbolic system of his own.

His almost mystical concern with the spiritual nature of mankind, and his fascination with oracles, dreams and astrology, was in many ways closer to ancient occult teachings than psychology.

In *Memories, Dreams, Reflections* he wrote that, 'The collective unconscious is common to us all; it is the foundation of what the ancients called "the sympathy of all things".' Amongst his writings he records numerous examples of personal `psychic' experiences. These include telepathy; prophetic dreams; visions; and even a ghost sighting.

Jung's theories are complex. Basically, however, he saw the human psyche in three parts: the conscious, personal unconscious, and collective unconscious. Powerful universal figures, called archetypes, dwell within both the personal and collective unconscious.

These archetypes surface in myths, fairytales and legends; they can also be seen in the images of the Major Arcana. Symbolic beings such as the fertile mother, the Empress; the authoritarian father, the Emperor; and the wise old man, the Hermit, are archetypal figures found in the Tarot.

These dream-like images, say Jungians, help unconscious knowledge to surface. When they appear in a Tarot reading, they combine to form a meaningful pattern which relates to the inquirer's current situation or difficulties. They also, like other serious oracles, reflect the deeply hidden underlying motives, fears and desires which can mould the individual destiny.

Divination and the Tarot

Tarot cards should never be regarded as a simple method for telling fortunes. Ordinary playing cards can be used for this purpose, and are better suited to the 'you will meet a tall, dark stranger' school of soothsaying.

The Tarot is, amongst other things, a tool for divination. It can be used to analyse problems, clarify the decision-making process, or even help you to understand yourself and others a little better. It can stimulate intuition, and help the mind to escape from the habitual straitjacket of logical thought into a more freewheeling world.

'Know Thyself' were the words carved above the entrance to the celebrated Delphic Oracle. Self-awareness is essential both when reading the cards for another, and when trying to understand what they are telling you personally. Self-knowledge and acceptance are what all forms of serious divination are really about.

When the cards are used to predict the future they can be uncannily accurate, but will invariably point to possibilities rather than probabilities. They also, if interpreted correctly, direct the inquirer's attention to the forces shaping his or her path in life – and often present choices, or suggest courses of action. This then places the responsibility for 'life, liberty, and the pursuit of happiness' firmly in the inquirer's own hands, where it ultimately belongs.

Synchronicity and prediction

Nobody really knows for certain how a set of cardboard pictures could possibly reveal anything about the present, let alone the future. Perhaps Jung's theory of synchronicity comes closest to giving us a quasi-scientific explanation.

Synchronicity crudely means 'meaningful coincidence', a term used by Jung and eminent physicist Wolfgang Pauli.

These two great minds collaborated in an attempt to define clusters of coincidences, which, they believed, were ultimately governed by some mysterious principle.

Most scientists would ascribe a series of mysterious or amazing coincidences to chance. But Jung believed that such events contain a meaningful message, because the more of them there are the more unbelievable they become. Therefore, there must be a purpose behind them, a guiding force which transcends that old scientific favourite, cause and effect.

So, when the cards are laid out, and are seen to form a pattern which makes complete sense to the inquirer, the law of synchronicity could be working behind the scenes. Or, if your prefer, it is simply an example of the old esoteric maxim 'as above, so below'; a minute part of the greater pattern is being revealed, as the veil of incomprehension is briefly twitched aside.

THE MAJOR ARCANA

Jung's theory of the archetypes is also linked to the very ancient idea of a 'world soul'. This was known to alchemists and other philosophers by its Latin name: anima mundi. The anima mundi – like the depth psychologists' collective unconscious – is said to be like a vast library.

—◆ ◆ ◆—

Contained within this imaginary library are all the world's experiences, philosophies and mystical ideas. These memories have been fed into the *anima mundi* by each and every living being since the world began.

As generation succeeds generation, we all – it is said – dip into and contribute to this complex collection of images. Archetypal figures are strengthened and refined, but because they represent the sum total of human experience, they remain fundamentally the same.

Some philosophers have asserted that it is possible for an individual to make direct contact with the *anima mundi* and learn from its wisdom. From this timeless pool spring our most enduring and numinous beliefs. When they influence us without our knowledge, they can wreak havoc, but when consciously approached, all the collected truths of the world may be at our disposal.

As we have seen, theories about the Major Arcana range from glamorous fantasy to scholarly investigation. In some ways, it does not matter where the images came from originally, for it seems that they sprang from a deep level. Arguably, those who are actively creative, are drawing on this collective pool for their insights. This is why their images or writings affect other people, for at some level everyone recognises their power. It is the same with the Major Arcana; it affects most people who see it. Those who approach the Tarot with on open mind will sooner or later confront the forces represented by the archetypes. Their presence may be discerned in the destiny of individuals as implacable forces, coincidences and twists of fate.

Through the Tarot, especially the Major Arcana, experienced readers can glimpse the greater design behind a series of events; they are in touch with the *anima mundi*. By learning to work with these energies, both inquirer and diviner can develop and mature.

0
THE FOOL

PLANET: URANUS

'O'er rough and smooth she trips along,
And never looks behind;
And sings a solitary song
That whistles in the wind.'

Lucy Gray William Wordsworth

Above: The Fool from the Marseilles deck

Myths and symbols

The Fool is far from being 'foolish' in the modern sense of the word. This androgynous figure represents the sacred child, holy fool and protected medieval jester who could make fun of the king with impunity. Most decks depict him/her in the act of stepping off a cliff, seemingly oblivious to danger. Yet the Fool will always survive; a miracle will happen and he will go on to complete his journey through all the lessons represented by the Major Arcana.

The number of this card is zero, which stands for the continuous cycle of life, birth and death. Symbolically, the Fool is forever newly born and about to begin his search for the holy grail of spiritual enlightenment. He sets out on this perilous journey filled with hope and believing that anything is possible.

Astrologically, the Fool is an airy card linked with the planet Uranus. This planet governs independence, eccentricity, sudden flashes of intuition, freedom and inventiveness. It is also the planet of sudden changes, an association which is more appropriate to 16, the Tower. However, the unorthodox and creative influence of Uranus can be a powerful tool for change, and the Fool is a card of new beginnings.

The combined message of both planet and card suggests the kind of inspiration which springs from the subconscious, and should not be ignored. The Fool represents the optimistic child within us all who has not been restricted by conventional beliefs. Because he has yet to learn the meaning of fear, self-consciousness or doubt, he is unafraid of adventure and insecurity.

Interpretation

Let go, take a risk and don't worry about what other people think. You are protected by your optimism and innocence, and however mad your plans might seem you are very much in tune with yourself. This is the start of an exciting journey, which may be mental, physical, spiritual or all three – look to the surrounding cards for further illumination.

When the Fool represents an individual, he or she is likely to have some noticeably child-like characteristics or be about to behave in a spontaneous way. Someone unconventional could come into your life. Depending upon your own character, you may find this threatening or hugely enjoyable.

Whatever your reaction, this person can show you how to throw the rule book out of the window and take a fresh look at things. 'Lateral' thinking is the Fool's forte, and he or she could come up with some surprising solutions to your problems – or inspire you to have a brain-storming session yourself.

In terms of health and general energy, the Fool denotes nervous tension; great but undisciplined mental energy; and unstable conditions of all kinds. Since the Fool is both male and female it can signal sexual ambivalence, or an unconventional sex life. It can refer to someone with a very variable libido; bisexuality or homosexuality.

Reversed

Here is a warning to look before you leap. This is not the time to take a risk, change your job, or trust anyone you don't know very well. You, or someone close, may be a gambler. The Fool counsels you to hang on to your money, for luck has temporarily deserted you. If you are beginning a romantic relationship, take it slowly; your new lover may be thoughtless and flighty – wait a while before committing yourself.

If you are already involved with someone you may find it hard to pin the person down. You might want commitment, while he or she seems to need a great deal of freedom. Perhaps the person is younger than you, mentally or physically. Do not make yourself unhappy by trying to change him or her; you must either accept inherent eccentricities or forget the relationship – for it will never bring you the stability you seek.

Below: The Fool from the Waite deck

1

THE MAGICIAN

PLANET: MERCURY

'... in practice the magic art may be employed for the benefit either of individuals or of the whole community... the public magician occupies a position of great influence, from which, if he is a prudent and able man, he may advance step by step to the rank of a chief or king'

The Golden Bough Sir James Frazer

Myths and symbols

The Magician, shaman, witch, or wizard played a vital role in ancient societies all over the world. Whether healing, looking into the future, protecting people from negative forces, or presiding over fertility rituals, these specially-chosen people mediated between our world and the mysterious realms of the spirits. This work not only required highly-developed pyschic abilities, but demanded rigorous training as well.

The Magician has studied long and hard; his or her efforts have required will-power and creativity and have been rewarded, for this figure is very much in control of his or her path in life. Traditionally, the Magician wears the figure-eight symbol for eternity

above his head, and is shown presiding over a table. On the table there is a cup, pentacle or disc, sword and wand – the symbols of the four suits of the Minor Arcana.

These symbols are found in a number of ancient mythologies: Nemesis, Greek goddess of Fate, had the wand, cup, wheel and sword as her symbolic possessions. The four magical treasures of Celtic mythology were the Cauldron of Regeneration, Stone of Sovereignty, Spear of Lug and the Sword of Nuada. Each represents an aspect of life, personality, and knowledge. Like Nemesis, the Magician has control over these elements, and can rearrange them or use them as it suits him.

The Magician's designated planet, Mercury, serves to emphasize the magical ability to travel between two worlds. Hermes – as Mercury was known to the Greeks – was called the Psychopomp, who conducted souls into the underworld. Unlike them, he had the freedom to come and go as he pleased. Hermes / Mercury was a messenger god, moving swiftly with the aid of his winged sandals and helmet.

He is god of the alphabet, languages, magical knowledge, medicine, crossroads, and tricksters. In medieval times he became the patron of alchemists, because of his legendary ability to turn things into gold with a touch of his caduceus. This is another obvious link with magic, which traditionally entails transformation through an effort of will. Astrologically, Mercury is the planet of communication, intellect, reason and teaching.

Interpretation

Initiating projects, having a sense of control over your destiny, and making creative ideas a reality are all possible when the Magician appears in a spread. The Fool's schemes and dreams can evaporate like morning mist without some practical, self-disciplined action.

The Magician helps you work towards achieving goals. You may be called upon to organize a department in an office, find yourself in a teaching role, or feel especially clear-sighted and logical. An interest in languages, writing, public speaking or psychotherapy is also suggested by this card.

When the Magician manifests in your life, he may be some kind of agent or entrepreneur who successfully brings together a number of different people or skills. He can represent someone who is witty, eloquent, and at home in the world.

Physically, the Magician is associated with the central nervous system, lungs, and the five senses. It is an unemotional card, sometimes suggesting someone who is not in touch with his or her feelings, or who over-analyses everything. Nervous exhaustion and breathing difficulties are the forms of illness linked to the Magician.

Like the Fool, this is an androgynous card. Sexually, this can indicate a perfect balance between male and female forces for it is a card of self-love, without which a relationship soon runs into difficulties. If you draw this card when you are interested in starting a relationship, do not be afraid to make the first move.

Below: The Magician from the Marseilles deck

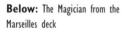

Above: The Magician from the Waite deck

Reversed

You are dithering about something, unable to make a choice. Perhaps positive and potentially successful plans have been abandoned, or you have been unwilling or unable to see things through to their conclusion. Sometimes these difficulties seem to have been caused by someone else. Certainly, some negative force or person is blocking your path and you may feel lacking in inspiration or energy.

2

THE HIGH PRIESTESS
or PAPESS

☽

PLANET: THE MOON

'And thou who thinkest to seek for me, know thy seeking and yearning shall avail thee not, unless thou knowest the mystery; that if that which thou seekest thou findest not within thee, then thou shall never find it without thee. For behold, I have been with thee from the beginning; and I am that which is attained at the end of desire.'

Charge of the Goddess from Witchcraft ritual

Myths and symbols

The High Priestess, sometimes known as the Papess, or Lady Pope, represents the virginal, self-contained aspect of the ancient Triple-Faced Goddess, ruled by the Moon. This goddess is linked to the cyclical phases of the Moon; in her virgin or maiden guise she is the New Moon; as the great and fertile mother, the Full; and as the infinitely-wise old Crone she is the dark and waning Moon.

The veiled face of the goddess represents mystery, secrets, and the eternal ebb and flow of the Moon's influence upon Earth and its creatures. The great Egyptian goddess Isis, in her veiled form, presided over a powerful and widespread mystery religion in ancient times. This extended all over Greece, Asia Minor, and had cult centres in Rome and Memphis. She offered salvation and regeneration after her death to her followers, and was known as myrionymos, 'the one with ten thousand names', since she incorporated aspects of many other goddess forms within her complex character.

Astrologically, the Moon represents mother, feelings, instincts, changeable moods, the feminine principle and fertility. All these qualities are combined in the High Priestess, daughter of the Moon, who guards the gateways to the deepest recesses of the mind.

Interpretation

When the High Priestess appears, she represents the sixth sense, heightened perception and a fascination with the unknown. She is telling you to look within, pay attention to your dreams, and listen to the inner voice we all possess and seldom use. She may appear at a time in your life when you are particularly interested in mystic subjects, the paranormal or occult. She can herald some hidden part of yourself which is about to surface; deeper emotions, or psychic powers, for example.

She invariably counsels patience, waiting for the right time, and relying on gut feelings rather than logical answers. Her secrets will be revealed eventually; you may not be ready to understand them yet. This is a good time to learn how to develop your intuition, try divination, or use creative visualization techniques.

Above left: The High Priestess from the Marseilles deck (and **right:**) from the Waite deck

seasonal temperature fluctuations.

The High Priestess has no need of men, and in certain circumstances can represent lesbian sexuality. Within a heterosexual relationship, she signifies female mystery and can mean that, for a woman, the man in your life does not really understand you. This card also suggests emotional isolation, brought on by a tendency to confide only in other women. This may leave a male partner feeling resentful and rejected.

When she represents a person, she may be your mother – especially if she is widowed, divorced or alone in life. She can appear as a psychic woman, witch or powerful female boss.

In a man's cards she can symbolize the sometimes frightening female aspects of himself, or manifest as a strong, independent woman whom he is unable to control or dominate. She can also represent an idealized lover, or distant woman he can never have a real relationship with because she has either rejected him, or is happy with someone else.

Physically, the High Priestess is associated with the element of water. In health matters she relates to body fluids, digestion, absorbing nutrients and clearing the body of poisonous wastes. She suggests an emotional sensitivity to the Moon, weather conditions, and

Reversed

Stand back, do not act immediately, but take the time to look carefully at your problems. There is a lot going on beneath the surface when the High Priestess appears upside down, consequently this is not the right time to proceed. Since you are not in full possession of all the facts you must wait until they emerge.

This position may also indicate that you have repressed or ignored intuitive feelings, and warns you of the danger of this approach. Socially, you may be surrounded by shallow, superficial people.

The High Priestess reversed can sometimes warn of hidden enemies, usually female. Someone may be working against you, or feel jealous and destructive towards you. Watch your step, and keep your own counsel If you suspect this to be true.

3
THE EMPRESS

PLANET: VENUS

'Rise up, my love, my fair one, and come
away.
For lo, the winter is past, the rain is over
and gone;
The flowers appear on the earth; the time
of the singing of birds is come, and the
voice of the turtle is heard in our land.'
Song of Solomon (2:10)

Myths and symbols

The Empress represents the fertile Mother Goddess, who was worshipped all over the ancient world. She is linked with the great silver disc of the Full Moon, at the height of its monthly cycle. Her womb was the earth itself, and her children were the edible fruits of the earth, which sustained life. Without her help, mankind believed that there would be an endless, barren winter with no hope of spring.

Her most enduring symbol is the ear of corn, which appears in various forms on many Tarot cards depicting the Empress. Another important symbol is the 'Madonna' lily, whose starry shape reflected the fact that many of her names meant star: Astarte, Ishtar, and Eostre (Easter) being some of the best–known. For the same reason, the Empress is sometimes shown crowned with stars.

This card is associated with Venus, planet of love, harmony, union and beauty. In astrology, Venus rules Taurus, an earth sign, and Libra, an air sign. Here Venus reveals her earthy, sensual face. The Taurean Venus is concerned with the earth, its special smell after rain has fallen, beautiful overflowing gardens, luscious ripe fruits. Sensuality is expressed through a healthy appetite for food and sex; a love of tactile fabrics such as velvet and silk; massage with perfumed oils; and rich colours in clothes and furnishings.

Interpretation

The Empress represents powerful female forces. When symbolizing a state of mind, she is telling you that you are brimming over with creativity. The time is right for you to expand and grow. Financially and materially you will be well provided for, and your basic needs will be comfortably met.

If you are an artist of any kind you will be able to draw on the practical energy required to paint, write, sculpt. If your question is related to career, this card directs your attention towards this area, or anything that is associated with beauty, such as hairdressing, massage, exercise, aromatherapy, or skin care.

Your creative impulses may also express themselves in cooking, gardening, or the urge to make your home a more beautiful place. Ideally, every idea must be conceived, nurtured, and ultimately given birth to. This is the essence of the Empress, who denotes

Right: The Empress from the
Marseilles deck

growth and birth. These
concepts may apply to a
physical baby, business,
work of art or love rela-
tionship.

When signifying a
person, the Empress
stands for a warm, loving
and sensual woman. She
may represent a man's
great love, the woman he
wants to share his life
with. She may enter your
life as someone strong
and caring; someone who is creative;
someone who is intensely alive and
enjoys life to the full. This person will
stimulate these qualities in you, for the

Empress means abundance,
sunshine and harvest on
every level.

Physically, this card often
foretells a pregnancy or
birth. You are fertile, and
highly receptive.

Harmonious sexual relationships are indicated, with
special emphasis on the
physical expressions of love
and affection.

Reversed

Your creativity and ability to
bring things to fruition is
blocked. Surrounding cards should indicate why. You may experience frigidity,
impotence or other sexual difficulties;
infertility may be a problem. Sex without
love, or meaningless promiscuity can
also be suggested. An unwanted child
may be conceived at this time; there is
the possibility of an abortion.

On a material level, the Empress
reversed can signify a period of poverty,
or other material discomfort. This card
has particular relevance to home comforts, your home may cease to be a
refuge under this influence. Perhaps you
discover damp, or noisy and disruptive
building work begins next door. Even if
you have enough money, you may feel
impoverished.

Spiritually, you are living through a
hard and icy winter. However, it is in the
nature of the Empress to return from
the underworld each spring; when she
falls in the reversed position she may
need a little help from you.

Above: The Empress from the Waite deck

4
THE EMPEROR

SIGN: ARIES

'Begin at the beginning', the King said, gravely, 'and go on till you come to the end; then stop.'

Alice in Wonderland Lewis Carroll

Myths and symbols

An essentially masculine card, the Emperor stands for the father gods of mythology, who had dominion over the skies. The Greek Zeus hurling his thunderbolts from Mount Olympus, or Scandinavian Thor wielding his great hammer are two manifestations of this principle.

Zeus gave birth to Athene, goddess of war and wisdom, from his own head – symbolizing the ascent and development of logic, reason, and authority. Such concepts are traditionally masculine in nature, belonging – according to numerous researchers – to the left brain, while the right is 'female', creative, and instinctive by nature.

This card is associated with Aries, the first sign of the zodiac, ruled by Mars, god of war. Aries is very much a dynamic 'go out and get' sign, connected with initiating projects, leadership, and power. In the Tarot, these qualities are modified by the Emperor's number which is four. Here four-square stability, foundation, and a firm structure are represented. This solid base channels and contains the extrovert, fiery qualities of Aries making long-term achievement a real possibility.

Interpretation

The Emperor represents structure, and the kind of power which arises from it. He symbolizes worldly achievement, and the competitive qualities and drive it takes to make your mark. When you draw the Emperor you may be on the verge of promotion, or be in a position where others look to you for direction. You are ambitious, and can make logical plans to ensure your success.

Above: The Emperor from the Marseilles deck

You could be dealing with authority in some shape or form: large companies, governments, authorities and bosses are all typical manifestations of the Emperor. He can also represent your father, or anyone who plays that role in your life.

In terms of career, The Emperor signifies that you prefer to be boss and are not a natural employee. Specific work areas include science, politics, computers, the armed forces, and any job where you are in control – or where there is a recognizable hierarchy within which you can advance.

The Emperor can appear in your life as a successful and usually wealthy businessman. If your question concerned a relationship, then you may be involved with someone who finds it difficult to express emotions. This type of person is unwilling to let down defences, for he or she likes to be in control at all times.

If you asked about a man, he has been taught that 'big boys don't cry' and has repressed his feminine side. Of course, he has emotions – they just don't show very often. If your question concerned a woman, she may be financially successful but have little time to relax and be receptive.

Physically, this card relates to the head, headaches, and accidents affecting that part of the body. Sexually, it is the card of the hunter and seducer of either sex who usually gets what he or she wants, and tends to dominate a partner. The Emperor's blocked emotions find an outlet in passionate sex, although partners may not feel particularly loved or cherished at other times.

Above: The Emperor from the Waite deck

Reversed

Other, apparently more powerful people seem to be in control of your destiny. Your hatred of authority may have drawn this negative force into your life; by learning to deal with regulations and structures you will free yourself.

If you are in a position of command, you are about to lose some of your authority. You feel drained, threatened, vulnerable. You are out of touch with your masculine side, lacking in ambition, or overshadowed by a dominant parent.

In relationships, business or friendship the Emperor can manifest as a cold, calculating individual who may be using you to achieve his or her own ends.

5

THE HIEROPHANT
or POPE

SIGN: TAURUS

'If the doors of perception were cleansed,
everything would appear to man as it is,
infinite.'

William Blake

Myths and symbols

The Hierophant, or Pope, is an extraordinary Tarot figure who does not simply represent the head of the Christian Church. 'Hierophant' is an Ancient Greek word meaning a priest who initiates, one who interprets the sacred mysteries. These men embodied the god on earth, and were believed to become vessels for his spirit in certain rituals. Similarly, the word 'pontiff' means 'bridge' – again, there is the idea of uniting, leading to, and making connections.

This card is ruled by Taurus, the Bull, which governs the second house of the natural zodiac. The second house is traditionally associated with the material world, possessions, money, and security. At first glance, these things seem very far from spiritual realms. However, belongings can say a lot about a person,

for they are an outward expression of an inner belief.

In ritual, whether magical or religious, outward signs can be very important. An especially beautiful place, richly-decorated robes, symbolic pictures and all the other outward trappings of religion can help to create atmosphere. In this way people can more easily direct their thoughts towards spiritual matters. Yet too much concentration on these things may have the opposite effect; some religions and spiritual movements have rejected opulence in favour of the utmost simplicity.

Interpretation

The High Priestess represents a gateway to hidden knowledge and ancient secrets. The Hierophant is also a gateway, but a more conventional one. When you draw this card, you may be going to university – as teacher or student. You, or someone close to you, may be very attracted to an orthodox religion, or need the strength and the certainty this can provide.

When this card signifies an aspect of personality, it suggests someone who pays great attention to outer details. A tidy home, a regular routine, and a dislike for anything which disrupts the even tenor of life are characteristic.

On the negative side, such an individual can be overly concerned about what other people think, maintaining the status quo, and 'keeping up with the Joneses'. He or she invariably has money in the bank, and disapproves of extravagant gestures.

Left: The Hierophant from the Waite deck

Right: The Hierophant from the Marseilles deck

Marriage is another meaning of this card. The solemn ceremony, with all its symbolic moments, is a profoundly important ritual in most societies. The Hierophant relates to the dramatic and traditional elements of marriage. Additionally, this card suggests the public joining together of two families, two sexes, two destinies.

When the Hierophant manifests as a person he or she may be a gifted teacher, priest, mentor, or interpreter. Such a person has entered your life to open some mental door for you, revealing what lies beyond. Whatever is taught, you will have a structure: language, astrology, music, and theology are typical subjects linked with the Hierophant. This card can also signify an old friend, often someone older than you, who is able to give you some sound advice.

You may feel a deep need for routine when you draw this card. You want to eat your meals at the same time every day; you find it difficult to think straight when things are in a state of uncertainty around you.

You also want your role defined clearly, whether in a relationship, or at work.

Reversed

The spirit of anarchy is alive and well and about to enter your life, or your thoughts. Rebellion against the establishment, breaking all the rules, and acting in an eccentric way are all suggested here.

Rules and regulations make you feel claustrophobic, you cannot see the point in them. You may turn against your background, and reject parental values. If you have been brought up in a conventional religious atmosphere you may turn your back on it now, and seek your own truths.

If you are seeking advice, particularly from a conventional source such as a lawyer or accountant, you would be wise to take a second opinion. You are in danger of judging a book by its cover, and being overly impressed by titles, or letters after someone's name. Do not rush into any new agreements. If buying expensive things for the home, they will prove disappointing.

6

THE LOVERS

SIGN: GEMINI

'My face in thine eye, thine in mine appears,
And true plain hearts do the faces rest,
Where can we find two better hemispheres
Without sharp North, without declining West?
Whatever dies, was not mixed equally;
If our two loves be one, or, thou and I
Love so alike, that none do slacken, none
can die.'

The Good Morrow John Donne

Myths and symbols

The Lovers invariably shows three figures. Sometimes there is a couple, with an angelic being hovering over them. Sometimes Cupid plays this role, and in other decks a young man is shown with two women – one young and one mature. These figures are often said to represent the conscious mind (male), unconscious (female) and the higher self (angel, cupid). In cards depicting two women, the older one may have been intended to represent the priestess who would marry the young couple. Women played a far from subservient role in ancient religions, including medieval Catharism.

This card is ruled by Gemini, the Twins. The Twins variously symbolize active and passive, light and dark, conscious and unconscious, positive and negative. The spiritual lesson of this sign is to learn how to blend these apparent opposites in what is effectively a mental and emotional marriage. This fusion can only be brought about through the powers of love, including physical love. Eastern philosophies such as Tantra and Taoism believed that sexual union was one of the true paths to enlightenment. They did not see the body as an obstacle, or as something disgusting, but as a temple of the spirit.

Interpretation

Not surprisingly, the Lovers suggests love, romance, and an emotional, spiritual and physical union. Any relationship connected to this card will be a powerful and meaningful one. The old idea of a soulmate is suggested here.

You may feel as if you have known one another always, be able to read each other's minds, and feel completely in tune on every level. Many occultists would say that you have been together before, loving through many different lifetimes in many different cultures. You are, quite simply, meant for each other.

Sometimes this card can mean an 'inner marriage'. In this case, you have resolved many conflicts within yourself, and are happy with your body. Your male and female characteristics are well-balanced at this time, your energy finds positive expression. Sexually, you are just as happy to initiate as to receive, and are full of affection.

The other important meaning of the Lovers is choice. If it appears when you are trying to make your mind up, it is telling you to think very carefully. Choices indicated by this card are not black and white, nor easily resolved in a logical way. Sometimes they are presented as two paths; you can continue with what you are currently doing, or take a risk and try something new.

You must use your intuition, and ask yourself a few questions. The Lovers counsels you to go wherever your heart leads you. Does your home, job, or relationship reflect you – or do you sometimes wonder what you are doing in one of these areas of life? Have you sacrificed your ideals completely? Look closely at your life, and think quietly about your question. If you feel you have sold out in order to gain security, please someone else, or because you are lazy, the Lovers offers you a chance to get back on the right path.

nership, or a gradual withdrawal of affection and commitment.

If you get this card at the beginning of an affair it serves as a warning. You may end up as one point in an eternal triangle, and emerge as the loser. You may be the victim of deception, or short-lived but powerful feelings. Do not make any irrevocable choices at this time.

Right: The Lovers from the Waite deck

Below: The Lovers from the Marseilles deck

Reversed

This position often denotes adultery, sex without love, and relationship difficulties. Within a relationship, it indicates a disrupted sex life. One partner may be trying to control the other, and using sex – or the lack of it – as a weapon. Anger and disharmony lurk just beneath the surface.

Jealousy could be a serious problem, driving a poisonous wedge between two people. One partner may feel shut out, neglected or frustrated emotionally and physically. These feelings are likely to result in an affair outside the part-

7

THE CHARIOT

SIGN: CANCER

'To travel hopefully is a better thing than
to arrive, and the true success is to labour.'

El Dorado R. L. Stevenson

Myths and symbols

A young hero or heroine stands boldly
upright in a splendidly-decorated
chariot, drawn by two creatures – one
black and one white. Yet this imposing
figure rarely has control of the reins,
if any are shown at all. The Chariot as
a symbol is found in many mythologies.
The Greek Sun god, Helios, rode his
chariot across the skies every day;
Roman Mars was often shown riding
in his chariot of war, while in India
the Lord of the World's great chariot
rumbled inexorably along the road of
time.

The creatures at the front of the
Chariot are usually said to symbolize
night and day, conscious and unconscious, past and present. By understanding and working with these
forces, one may come to terms with
duality, gain control, and in conse-
quence succeed.

The Chariot is very much about
tuning in with these cosmic cycles, and
realizing that they are often more powerful than ourselves. By going against
nature, we will ultimately fail and be
destroyed; in many ways the Chariot is
a card for our times. We have fought
nature, and briefly triumphed over her.
Now she is fighting back.

Linked with Cancer, the Crab, this
card also expresses the tenacity of that
sign. Crabs hang on tightly, do not give
up easily, and often make intuitive side-
ways moves. They are extremely self-
protective, for their tough outer shell
cradles a vulnerable, soft interior. Ruled
by the Moon, they are more aware than
most zodiacal signs of the shifting
nature of the universe.

Glory, success and honour are
changeable too. While the Chariot
speaks of victory, it also warns against
excessive pride.

Interpretation

You have put in a lot of hard work, and
are about to be rewarded. Your self-discipline may have been a struggle at
times, but you are coming into the
home straits and victory is in sight last.

You may experience 'overnight' success. Others will tell you how lucky you
are, but luck has little or nothing to do
with it. This kind of success has been
won after a battle – with yourself, or
obstacles in your path. You find yourself
acting in a theatrical success after years
of working in draughty, provincial theatres. Your book becomes a best–seller,
but only after it has been rejected by

Above: The Chariot from the Marseilles deck

twenty different publishers. You win a coveted promotion by working long hours, and sticking to your plans.

When the Chariot thunders into your life as a person, it represents someone who does not give up and who firmly believes in the motto, 'If at first you don't succeed, try, try again'. Such a friend can inspire you, too, for he or she will encourage you not to give in. This is a successful person, or one who is about to become so.

Sometimes the Chariot becomes a real physical vehicle. This vehicle brings news, or friends from far-flung places. In a more abstract way, it can bring you the energy and will-power to use your abilities to the full. Whatever gifts you have are meant to be used, even if this entails a struggle with yourself. Switch off the television (often a visual drug), says the Chariot, and get on with it.

Reversed

Addiction, envy and avarice. The Chariot reversed suggests negative attitudes, limitations and loss of self-control. You may think that the world owes you a living, or be very gifted but afraid to use your abilities. Perhaps talents come too easily, or arrogance, or lack of self-confidence are hindrances. This position can denote someone who buries his or her head in the sand, using drink or drugs as a way to dull the senses and forget about reality. Also it acts as a warning against overwhelming ambition, burning up energy, and wasting your resources.

Above: The Chariot from the Waite deck

8

STRENGTH

SIGN: LEO

'Out of the strong came forth sweetness.'

Judges (14.4)

Myths and symbols

Strength depicts a woman, usually in the act of opening a lion's mouth. Such an act requires courage and certainty, although in many decks the lion seems to be co-operating rather meekly. The figure-eight symbol for eternity is drawn over the woman's head, sometimes in the form of a hat.

The human figure is also intended to represent the conscious mind coming to terms with our instinctive, animal natures. Some experts maintain that the woman (in some, more recent decks – a man) is taming or controlling these forces which lurk deep within us all. Others suggest co-operation between the two.

This card is ruled by the solar sign of Leo, the Lion, which rules the fifth house of the natural zodiac. Positive attributes of this sign include honesty, generosity, loyalty and reliability. It is

Above: Strength from the Marseilles deck

this fixed sense of purpose, combined with high ideals, which pervades Strength; Leo rules the heart, physically and emotionally, while the fifth house is connected with creativity, romance, pleasure and children.

Interpretation

Strength does, of course, mean strength. But it has nothing to do with brute force or violence. This kind of strength comes from a generous, loving heart.

When you draw Strength, you have the courage of your convictions and will triumph over hatred, miserly attitudes, and mean-spirited enemies. You are filled with faith and power; optimism and a firm resolve will enable you to win through in any situation.

When Strength manifests as a person, he or she is generous and fair–minded. You may be the fortunate recipient of liberality, or encounter someone who will fight on your behalf. This person cannot stand by and see injustice or cruelty without trying to put things right. Such people will not acknowledge defeat or negativity and their considerable will-power and energy will inspire you.

If you have been involved in an unpleasant dispute, or have experienced antagonism from others, you will be able to resolve things now. Strength overcomes dark forces with the power of love, resistance crumbles and you are reconciled with your enemies.

Sometimes this card can translate itself quite literally. When this happens a beloved animal could enter your life. You will gain great pleasure from this association, and find the animal a soothing and healing influence. Animals love unconditionally, they do not judge you and find you wanting. This is the kind of love symbolized by this card.

If you draw Strength when you are experiencing relationship difficulties, you must try to open your heart, forgive and forget. All is certainly not lost, but a reconciliation demands love on both sides. Strength suggests that there is more than enough love between you; a happy future together is possible if you are both determined, and do not give up at the first hurdle.

Below: Strength from the Waite deck

Reversed

Courage has deserted you, you have lost your nerve and no longer believe that anything is possible. Fear and weakness are barriers to success; at this point these negative forces are barriers to achievement.

When this position represents a person it signifies he or she has given in, taken the easy way out, and accepted defeat. Fear of what the future holds may be the motive; fear has frozen the ability to act.

Sometimes this position is telling you to summon up your inner strength and carry on despite genuine difficulties. You will be successful if only you can overcome your fear of failure, enemies or obstacles.

9
HERMIT

SIGN: VIRGO

'That content surpassing wealth
The sage in meditation found,
And walked with inward glory crowned.'

P. B. Shelley

Myths and symbols

The Hermit, or religious recluse, is a familiar figure in many religions. He symbolizes the need to withdraw from the world for a while to contemplate the meaning of life, and seek enlightenment. By deliberately isolating himself, he is able to concentrate completely on union with spiritual powers.

A hermit retires to the wilderness, to the top of a lonely mountain, or finds a distant cave for his solitary home. Here, he learns inner wisdom and listens to the voice of his higher self. Most Hermits in the Tarot carry a lamp, symbolizing spiritual light and knowledge.

Hecate, the dark goddess of crossroads, witchcraft, and midwifery is the ancient female counterpart of the Hermit. Here is the third face of the Triple Goddess in her guise as a wise old woman, dark destructive mother, and crone. Hecate governed both the waters of the sea, and the waters of the womb when they broke during labour. She dwelt in the underworld, but often held a torch. The light from this torch illuminated the secrets of the unconscious, profound mysteries which are not easily revealed.

This card is paired with Virgo, the Virgin, which governs the sixth house of the natural zodiac. Virgo is traditionally the sign of work and service to others. These ideas are found in the Hermit, too, but here they also have a spiritual meaning. Selfless service is one way to rid ourselves of arrogance and conceit. As such, it is used by Buddhism and Christianity – amongst others – as a means of purifying the soul.

Nine is the number of the Hermit, a number of completion, creativity and the universe. The Fool has learnt many things on his journey; the next stage of initiation has been reached, and he must sit quietly for a time.

Interpretation

You have a pressing need to be by yourself in order to think, and make plans. You want to unplug the telephone, cancel social arrangements, and leave the door unanswered. Perhaps there is a serious decision to make; you may feel you have achieved everything you have set out to do and wonder what's next.

You will soon realize that there is always something new to learn, and may want to study philosophy, spiritual doc-

Above: The Hermit from the Marseilles deck

trines, or learn how to meditate. You may want to spend some time in a retreat; take long solitary walks; or travel alone. Peace and quiet are important now, and you will not lose out if you drop out of the social whirl for a time.

Sometimes the Hermit can enter your life as a teacher. This person is unlikely to be a conventional teacher, but will be someone wise and kind who can guide you in the right direction. Listen to the advice that is given, for it will be worth its weight in gold.

When the Hermit appears, it can be a warning against thoughtless action. This card's message is one of prudence, caution and discretion in worldly affairs. Take as much time as you need to reach your conclusions, and consider every angle. Silence is golden, says the Hermit, for it illuminates the path ahead.

Reversed

Many people hate being alone, and may experience this card as enforced loneliness. They need noise, distractions and ceaseless activity for they are frightened to look too deeply inside themselves. This position suggests immaturity and superficiality; a life full of empty chatter.

Try not to reject advice given to you if you receive this card. It will be sound, and you would be very foolish to ignore it. This position can sometimes indicate pig-headed obstinacy, and refusal to listen.

The Hermit reversed can also be telling you that you are wasting your time in some way; your energy could be used more productively. Examine your life and preoccupations.

Above: The Hermit from the Waite deck

10

THE WHEEL OF FORTUNE

♃

PLANET: JUPITER

'Free will is the ability to do gladly that which I must do.'

C. G. Jung

Myths and symbols

The Wheel of Fortune, Time, and Fate symbolizes the endless cycle of death and rebirth. In the Tarot, this wheel is often presided over by a sphinx-like figure – for the sphinx knew the secrets of Time. In each corner of the card there is usually one of four figures: a bull, lion, eagle and angel.

These symbols represent a number of things. Each one belongs to a fixed sign of the zodiac – the Angel to Aquarius; the Bull to Taurus; the Lion to Leo; and the Eagle to Scorpio. Four ancient pagan festivals fall during the time the Sun is passing through these signs. These are Imbolc or Candlemas on 2nd February; Beltane or May Day on 1st May; Lugnasad or Lammas on 1st/2nd August; and Samhain or Hallowe'en on 31st October/1st November.

These festivals, too, represent a journey. There is the journey through the seasons; seed-time, fruition, harvest, and withdrawal. There is also the journey of the goddess through all her phases; as maiden, bride, mother and crone. Each circular trip eventually returns to its starting point at Samhain, when the goddess departs for the underworld.

Modern interpreters have also allocated four psychological functions to these elemental creatures. The Bull, which belongs to the earth, represents feeling and our physical senses. The Lion, whose element is fire, stands for intuition. The Scorpion Eagle is associated with the emotional element of water. And the airborne Angel of Aquarius stands for intellect, and the mental faculties.

This card is traditionally linked with the planet Jupiter, sometimes known as the Luck Bringer, or Great Benefic. It is an expansive planet, striding through the zodiac like a favourite uncle dis-

Below: The Wheel of Fortune from the Marseilles deck

Above: The Wheel of Fortune from the Waite deck

pensing treats and happy surprises. Here, the sense of growth relates to both material circumstances and spiritual awareness. As the great Wheel of Fortune turns, so the soul learns to balance the four elements within.

Interpretation

The Wheel of Fortune focuses upon the difficult issue of destiny versus free will, an almost impossible question to solve. However, both factors seem to operate in life to varying degrees, depending on individual circumstances.

In my view, we are not at the mercy of Fate all the time. Destiny has provided us with certain talents, character traits, parental background and so on. But what we do with this material, and what we can learn from it seems to be up to us. There is usually a choice, or a point where one can make a decision. This is how we learn.

When you draw the Wheel, you are approaching one of those moments in life when Fate does take a hand in your affairs. Strange coincidences, fortunate meetings, and lucky breaks can all shape your destiny at this time. You may feel as if your life script has been written by someone else. You begin sentences with 'You'll never believe this, but...'. The Great Cosmic Joker is in a benevolent mood, and has decided to throw a few favours in your direction.

One thing is certain, the wheel has turned and you are beginning a new cycle. Positive confusion reigns. Although it may be difficult to live through, it is important not to resist this phase, for when the dust has settled you may find yourself with a whole new set of friends, a new career, or a totally-unexpected new home.

Reversed

Bad luck dogs your path. The goddess of fortune is wearing her dark and destructive face, there is a celestial spanner in the works.

Take heart, for the Wheel is always in motion and if you can be patient Fate will smile on you once more. This is a bad time to initiate any fresh projects, or gamble on things going in your favour.

Unexpected delays appear out of nowhere. You can still be heard to say 'You'll never believe this, but...'; this time bad news completes the sentence. Take comfort in the fact that change is usually positive in the end, and expect the unexpected.

11

JUSTICE

SIGN: LIBRA

'Order is heaven's first law.'

Alexander Pope

Myths and symbols

The card of balance, Justice depicts a female figure holding the scales and sword. This figure is still a familiar one, although she is usually blindfolded nowadays. In Ancient Egyptian mythology the goddess Maat weighed the souls of the dead against her Feather of Truth. Her name means truth and justice, which were thought to form the basis of an ordered universe.

Other cultures saw her as Fate incarnate, who presided over the laws of karma – or cause and effect – and dealt out retribution or honours accordingly.

Libra, sign of the scales, is associated with this card. Libra is concerned with harmony and balance – particularly of a mental kind. Because it is an airy sign it relates primarily to the mental realms, and mental balance rather than emotional concerns. Libra governs the seventh house of the natural zodiac, the house of partnership.

There is some dispute about the true position of Justice in the Tarot. Some experts suggest that she should be placed in the eighth position, between the assertive Charioteer and the introspective Hermit. This would then give a message of balance between the inner and outer worlds.

The number eight is associated with the idea of justice; there is an old belief that there were eight blessings for the chosen, and eight punishments for the damned. Eleven suggests that luck and prosperity will come out of adversity, and could therefore be considered more appropriate for Strength.

Placing Justice between the Chariot and the Hermit also denotes the transitory nature of worldly glory, or attachment to material values. Inner development must be accomplished too, or Fate may weigh you in her scales and find you lacking in humility.

Some modern decks have replaced Justice in the eighth position; in others you will find this card numbered eleven. The Waite deck, which is illustrated opposite, places Justice in the eleventh position, while the card is numbered eight in the Marseille deck, (also illustrated opposite) and in the Hanson-Roberts and Barbara Walker decks.

Interpretation

Justice can sometimes indicate a choice or decision. This kind of decision is primarily logical, and can be worked out accordingly. A list of pros and cons

Right: Justice from the Marseilles deck

should soon make the choice clear; a sharp mind is what is required when you draw this card.

Psychologically, you are balanced, with a fair, clear-sighted view of life. You are not overdoing things in any area, or neglecting some part of your life in favour of another.

Justice often appears in answer to questions connected with the law, contracts, or formal agreements. This card can symbolize important legal documents, requiring signature, a court case, or negotiations. It can indicate accountants, judges, solicitors, union leaders and people who make laws.

When Justice manifests as a person, you can expect him or her to be involved in this type of career, or possess the type of mind ideally suited to calm, logical negotiation.

If you are currently involved with some kind of litigation, Justice suggests that the matter will be resolved in your favour. However, if you are making unreasonable demands or being greedy then you may get less than you hope.

Reversed

Injustice, imbalance and delays. Any legal process in your life will be slow and painful. You may have to pay more than you bargained for, or wait for a long time until your case is finally resolved. If you are getting divorced, there may be an unfair judgment against you in court. If you are buying a house, be prepared for complicated negotiations and much correspondence. Tax matters may be confused.

Emotionally, you may separate from your partner – especially if you are legally married. This kind of parting is unlikely to be very messy, or filled with recriminations. You could both decide that the time has come to part, and be able to do so on a fairly friendly basis.

Below: Justice from the Waite deck

12

THE HANGED MAN

PLANET: NEPTUNE

'I know I hung on that windy tree,
Swung there for nine long nights,
Wounded by my own blade,
Bloodied for Odin,
Myself an offering to myself:
Bound to the tree
That no man knows
Whither the roots of it run.'

The Speech of the High One from the Old Norse,
The Poetic Edda (ca. AD 1200)

Myths and symbols

The Hanged Man is one of the most powerful and disturbing images in the entire Tarot. He is often cited as unmistakable evidence of pagan meanings behind the cards, for he is not hung in an ordinary way. The Hanged Man dangles by one foot from a tree, he looks perfectly calm and is not in pain.

The Norse god, Odin, hung himself like this for nine nights on the world tree. At the end of this ritual sacrifice he was granted great wisdom in the form of the runes. Odin was a many-faceted god who presided over magic and inspiration, journeys, battle, and the realms of the dead.

In his role as the great magician and shape-shifter he has special relevance to the Hanged Man. He was credited with the power to create mental paralysis at critical moments; conversely, he could free the human mind from fear and hesitation. This, in essence, is the double message of the Tarot card, which can point to either or both of these states.

Yogis, too, have been turning themselves upside down for more than a thousand years. By standing on their heads in the famous pose known as the Sirsasana they believe they can activate the brain's nerve centres, and improve mental alertness.

This card is linked with Neptune, planet of dreams, artistic inspiration, mysticism and sacrifice. Here, its dissolving, watery influence suggests surrendering outworn concepts and fears in order to gain knowledge. The Hanged Man experiences spiritual ecstasy, too, for the ultimate meaning of this card is rebirth and regeneration. Pagan corn gods, like John Barleycorn, had to die in order to allow this regeneration to take place. Yet the sacrifice was willingly made.

Interpretation

You may feel unable to move forward or back when you receive the Hanged Man. Don't try, for you have reached a temporary pause in your life, and will be unable to effect changes now. You cannot make any sensible decisions, since you will probably be waiting for news or others' opinions and actions.

Patience is one of the traditional virtues, so try to cultivate it and enjoy

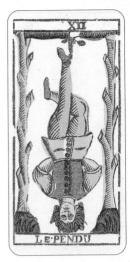

Above: The Hanged Man from the Marseilles deck

your waiting-room for you will not be in it forever.

The Hanged Man also suggests the notion of sacrifice. Something must be given up to gain something else. You may have to abandon a secure but boring job in order to gain a more fulfilling career. Perhaps things seem stale your relationship, or you feel trapped. In this case you need to give up your ideas about what a relationship should be, abandon convention and turn everything upside-down for a while.

Sometimes the 'sacrifice' has been made for you, and a special person, home or meaning in your life has been lost. This card may appear when someone is mourning an aspect of his or her life. There is hope. Emergence from this difficult period with renewed energy will occur sooner or later.

If your question involved a decision, this is not the right time to take it. Even if you go ahead, you will encounter delays. Accept that time is suspended, and that waiting is inevitable just now.

Reversed

When the Hanged Man falls in a reversed position, he warns the inquirer against selfishness and materialism. Events may run away with you, with disastrous results, unless you stop and think. Or you may be so busy hanging on to what you've got that you fail to grasp an opportunity when it arises. This card can also warn of bad investments, loss of belongings, and reversals of fortune.

You, or someone in your life, may be oppressing someone else. Do you feel like an unwilling victim, or is someone trying to manipulate you in some way? You may be pressurizing someone unwittingly in your eagerness to get things done. The Hanged Man advises you to stop what you are doing, remember the lessons of the Hermit, and consider your actions.

Below: The Hanged Man from the Waite deck

13

DEATH

SIGN: SCORPIO

'For that which is born death is certain,
and for the dead birth is certain.
Therefore grieve not over that which is
unavoidable.'

Bhagavad-Gita

Myths and symbols

Death, the grim reaper, is often portrayed as a skeletal figure with a scythe
in the Tarot, and in art. This image
played an important role in medieval
art, while death is allocated a significant
place in all the world's mythologies,
seen by some cultures as a mistake, by
others as a punishment for our sins, or
as an agreement between the first man
and the first woman. Behind these stories lies the idea that, long ago, people
could renew themselves and that death
was a temporary state of affairs.

In Hindu mythology, the goddess of
death is Kali the Destroyer. She is portrayed wearing a crown of severed
heads or a necklace of skulls. carrying
the sword of death, scissors to cut life's
thread, and – significantly – the lotus of
eternal generation, symbolizing the
endless cycles of death and rebirth. The
name Kali means 'Time'. Time often
accompanies Death in myth, while in
western art Death's scythe also belongs
to Father Time.

St Paul was not alone in thinking of
death as an enemy to be vanquished. In
I Corinthians, chapter 15, he said 'the
last enemy that shall be destroyed is
death'. A Coffin Text from ancient
Egypt suggested a similar attitude: 'Save
me from the claws of him who takes for
himself what he sees: may the glowing
breath of his mouth not take me away.'

Remnants of a more positive, celebratory attitude towards death linger in
the traditional Irish wake; the Mexican
Day of the Dead; and countless stories
of resurrection and rebirth.

Astrologically, Death is associated
with the sign of Scorpio and the eighth
house of the zodiac wheel. Scorpio is an
emotional and intuitive sign, traditionally linked with secrets, being both
secretive and intent on delving beneath
the surface to reveal the truth.
Scorpio's house is said to be the house
of sex, death, birth and transformation.
Transformation is the key-word here,
applying to both the Tarot card and its
astrological counterpart.

The number thirteen is popularly
held to be unlucky. It is the number of
witches in a coven, and the number of
lunar months in a year. According to an
old book on numerology it is the
number of death, destruction, faith,
hope and re-birth: 'He hath the key of
power and dominion who understands
the number 13'.

Above left: Death from the Marseilles deck (and **right:**) from the Waite deck

This card cannot be taken lightly. Major changes lie ahead, and you may require time to mourn what you are leaving behind. Think of it in terms of life itself; each phase serves its purpose and we move on to the next.

Death in the Tarot promises a new life once you are free of the old one. Occasionally it does augur physical death, but this rarely – if ever – applies to the querent. Never predict an actual death when you are reading the cards, it is a totally irresponsible thing to do.

This card can also signify a loss: a relationship fails; a friendship comes to an end, a job is lost. However, you should not despair. Something has fulfilled its allotted span in your life, and you must look forward to fresh horizons with hope and faith in the future.

Interpretation

More than any other Tarot image, Death is frightening to both inexperienced reader, and anxious querent. Most people are afraid of death, so many modern interpretations of this card suggest that it means 'change'. But the idea of confronting something implacable and alarming must not be completely brushed under the carpet.

When you draw this card it is certain that something is coming to an end. This experience may be painful, and difficult to come to terms with. Resistance to this change may work for a time, but not for ever. There is no need to fear; Death promises that transformation will follow. Some old and outworn part of yourself is dying, and your circumstances will eventually reflect this.

Reversed

You are resisting changes and this refusal to adapt is creating a stagnant atmosphere around you. You may feel lacking in energy, as if carrying some great weight. or wading through treacle.

Life could be very boring when you draw Death reversed. Nothing seems to have changed for a long time, everything seems to have lost its meaning . Lethargy and inertia poison your days, and you are so tired you cannot be bothered to do anything about it.

If surrounded by positive cards, Death reversed could be telling you to wait. Make the most of this quiet patch. You will overcome your fears, be released from the past, and sooner or later begin a new cycle.

14
TEMPERANCE

SIGN: SAGITTARIUS

'That which is below is like unto that which is above, and that which is above is like unto that which is below, to achieve the wonders of the One Thing.'

From *The Emerald Tablet* of HermesTrismegistos

Myths and symbols

Temperance depicts a female figure pouring water from one vessel into another. Sometimes this figure is a woman, sometimes an angel of indeterminate sex. The symbolic key to this card seems to lie in the name, and the idea of fluid flowing from one container to another.

Most people today associate the word temperance with abstention from alcohol, or moderation. But it has other, older meanings which would have been in common use when the cards were originally designed. *Temperare* in Latin means to moderate, mix, blend or otherwise bring into harmony; the angel seems to be blending the contents of her two vessels, rather than abstaining from a quick drink down at the local bar.

Sometimes this card was known as Time, which mends all wounds and marches on despite our efforts to put back the clock. *Tempore* in Latin means 'in the time of'; we use the word tempo to mean time in music. And as time passes the lessons of life symbolized by the Tarot unfold.

The liquid symbolizes the flow of life; the essential connection between conscious and unconscious; and the blending of male and female elements without which life would not continue. This balancing of male and female is a recurring theme in the Tarot, and indeed in ritual magic, psychology, and many spiritual doctrines. Here are the left and right sides of the brain, representing logic and intuition. Yin and Yang, light and dark, hot and cold – each requires its opposite to form a whole.

Temperance is numbered fourteen, a number of the moon. On the fourteenth day of her cycle the moon is exactly midway between new and full. The fourteenth day of a woman's menstrual cycle generally falls during her fertile time, when by blending with the opposite sex she is likely to become pregnant.

The ancient Assyrians held special rituals on the seventh, fourteenth and twenty-first days of the moon's cycle, and it is thought by a number of scholars that they were honouring their goddess's menstrual cycle in this way. An old numerology text states that the number fourteen 'controls continuous change, movement, and combination. It is the number of energy, sexuality and revolution.'

Temperance is associated with Sagittarius, the sign symbolized by a centaur – half man, half horse. This image also represents blending – animal and human nature are combined. Sagittarius is the great fiery seeker of the zodiac, who searches for meaning above and beyond normal everyday experience. Sagittarius rules the ninth house of the zodiac which is the house of far horizons; philosophy; higher education; and religion in the broadest sense.

Interpretation

Temperance brings a balanced, adaptable influence into your life. You are able to see both sides of an argument , and so resolve matters. You feel calm, in control of events, and able to take whatever fate throws your way.

If you have been involved in a dispute or disagreement you will be able to sort it out. This applies to personal or work problems. Temperance settles union disputes; negotiates acceptable wage increases; helps a couple overcome their differences and 'kiss and make up'.

This is excellent if you are involved in creative work, or have been looking for new ways to approach a project.

When Temperance represents a person, or aspect of character it suggests someone who works well in a team. A well-rounded personality is indicated, an excellent manager. This is the card of the diplomat, alchemist, and the calm voice in the storm suggested by 13, Death, and 15, the Devil.

Reversed

Things are out of balance. There are quarrels and disagreements. An atmos-

phere of restless competitiveness pervades group endeavours; this may stem from those around you or you could be feeling this way yourself.

You may feel as if there are not enough hours in the day. Temperance reversed warns of trying to do too much, scattering your energy, and becoming imbalanced as a result.

Depending upon the card's position, it could be referring to someone in your life who is behaving like this.

This card also signifies poor judgment; a balanced view of events is unlikely to be achieved, and decisions that are taken now may be regretted later.

Emotionally, you and your partner could be competing with one another in the same line of work. Perhaps one – or both – of you is restless, and cannot settle to anything. The more stable partner may feel as if he or she is living with a jumpy and unpredictable creature. Arguments are likely.

Below: Temperance from the Waite deck

15
THE DEVIL

SIGN: CAPRICORN

'What was he doing, the great god Pan,
Down in the reeds by the river?
Spreading ruin and scattering ban,
Splashing and paddling with hoofs of a goat,
And breaking the golden lilies afloat
With the dragon-fly on the river.'

A Musical Instrument Elizabeth Barrett Browning

Myths and symbols

A dancing horned figure surrounded by animals is depicted upon the walls of the Trois Freres cave in France – a Paleolithic image of the great horned god, Lord of the Animals, who was later turned into the devil. This god goes under many names, while his animal horns are most commonly those of a stag, goat, or bull. By the Middle Ages, he had come to symbolize Satan – supposed god of the witches, enemy of Christianity, and embodiment of evil.

In classical myth, he appeared as Pan the merry, goat-footed son of Hermes who wandered in high, rocky places and danced with nymphs in the forests. The rather rumbustious cult of Dionysus was also associated with goats, for goat-legged satyrs were amongst his fol-

lowers. These gods were connected with fertility, abandoned behaviour, and exuberant enjoyment in the form of noise, music, drinking and revelry of every kind. The English word 'panic' stems from the god Pan; the word pan derives from the Greek *pas* meaning 'all'.

The Devil is linked with the astrological sign Capricorn, which is symbolized by a fish-tailed goat. This sign rules the tenth house of the zodiac, the house of status, career, material needs and responsibilities.

Capricorn, often considered a dour and responsible sign, is not all duty and hard work. People born under Capricorn can have a deeply sensuous streak, enjoying wealth and the comforts and pleasures this can bring. In addition, Capricorn rules the time of year when the 'Lord of Misrule' was said to be abroad; this jolly pagan figure has much in common with Pan, and his lesser manifestation Puck – another tricksy, ancient nature spirit.

Interpretation

When the Devil appears in your cards there is no need to shudder, or believe that evil forces are around. This card basically represents the material world, which is neither good nor evil in itself.

You may be entering a phase when money, and material well-being become important. Perhaps you have rejected these things before, and are tired of never having enough money. You may start saving or collecting antiques or other beautiful objects. There is nothing wrong with this, as long as it does not

Above left: The Devil from the
Marseilles deck (and **right:**) from the Waite deck

become an obsession which takes over your life and thoughts.

Emotionally, the Devil warns against trying to buy friendship or love. There is a danger that you, or someone in your life will use money as a means of controlling others. In our society money does often mean power, and this card suggests that this influence could be entering your life.

Sometimes the Devil signifies someone who is overly concerned with material security. These worries may be preventing greater fulfilment, by keeping him or her trapped in a relationship or job – bound by apparent success.

If other cards, or your question, concerned a relationship, then tread carefully. The Devil, like his mythological ancestors, is inextricably linked with lust and sometimes overwhelming physical desire. Such powerful sexual attraction may be irresistible, but it may not

be love. You could find yourself obsessed by the object of your desire, or vice versa. You should certainly learn something about your own animal nature, but a lasting partnership may not necessarily be the outcome of this union.

Reversed

A serious warning against the abuse of power, money, sex, or personal charm. You, or someone in your life, have become greedy, egocentric, materialistic. In your career, money and power may have taken precedence over any other considerations. There is always more money to be made, greater power or position to be striven for. Depression could be a problem, yet you are on a treadmill of your own creation.

Emotionally you may be in thrall to someone who is not doing you any good. You feel unable to break away from this relationship, even while you know it is making you unhappy. You cannot explain your actions to concerned friends or family, for the magnetic pull this person has for you is illogical and you are under his or her spell.

You may also be in a difficult situation with a former lover. He or she may resort to some kind of emotional blackmail in an attempt to win you back.

Sexually, the Devil reversed is a shadowy card which many interpreters link to the far, wild shores of sexual behaviour. If your question concerned a sexual relationship, this card suggests that some exotic fantasies are about to be acted out.

16

THE TOWER

PLANET: MARS

'It is the business of the future to be dangerous... The major advances in civilization are processes that all but wreck the societies in which they occur.'

Adventures in Ideas Alfred North Whitehead

'Security is the mother of danger and the grandmother of destruction.'

Thomas Fuller

Myths and symbols

The Tower, or House of God is also sometimes known as the Tower of Destruction; the Lightning-Struck Tower or the Tower of Babel Blasted. It is a dramatic, apocalyptic image.

This symbol is perhaps most obviously linked to the Biblical story of the Tower of Babel, which was intended by its builders to reach heaven. These people, descendants of Noah, planned to invade God's domain to avenge their ancestors who were drowned in the legendary Flood. This never happened, for God caused them all to speak different languages and so they were unable to communicate with one another.

Lightning itself is associated with both wrath and destruction, and fertility and inspiration in myth. Zeus, the father of the gods, hurled thunderbolts around, demonstrating his power. The Devil, as Lucifer the fallen angel, was also believed to use lightning to strike at church towers, something he was rather successful at.

In traditional Aborigine belief, the Lightning Snake precedes the Great Mother by bringing the all-important wet season: 'When he raises his lengthening body from the springs, billabongs and rivers to the sky, flashing and roaring, the rains and floods come, and with them the wet season and the promise of life and increase for nature and man.' In the Tarot, the Tower precedes the Star – a card which represents the feminine principle very clearly.

Both Tower and lightning are masculine symbols, as is the planet linked to this card, Mars. An assertive, aggressive planet, Mars represents energy and activity. As a god, Mars was the Roman god of war who formerly protected crops and animals from storms, droughts and pestilence.

Interpretation

Exhilarating change is about to turn your life upside-down. At first, this may seem disruptive, even violent – for the Tower carries revolutionary overtones. Yet this change is necessary and positive, for it brings freedom and enlightenment in its wake.

The changes signified by the Tower may take a number of forms. They can come from deep within the psyche, denoting a radical upheaval of beliefs, values, or behaviour. These new ways of thinking may seem sudden, or even frightening for they are likely to erupt into con-

Above left: The Tower from
the Waite deck (and **right:**) from the Marseilles deck

been in a rut, and this upheaval is giving you a chance to climb out of it.

When the Tower refers to a relationship you are warned that things cannot carry on as before. Perhaps this association was not based on real feelings, or one of you was simply stringing the other along. If the relationship has a strong and enduring foundation it will be transformed for the better, although you may expect a bumpy ride before things settle down.

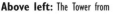

sciousness without much prior warning.

Sometimes the Tower suggests anger, and you may find yourself on a very short fuse under its influence. This is particularly true if you are someone who normally tries to keep the peace, repressing your own temper in the process.

This card can also indicate a swift change of home. You may decide to sell, a buyer walks in the next day and you find the home you want with similar speed. Within a couple of months you are living somewhere else, and attempting to catch your breath.

In terms of career, the changes are no less dramatic. You may suddenly hand in your notice; a new and unexpected source of income manifests 'out of the blue'; you are suddenly inspired to train for a new career, shocking friends and family. You may even find yourself redundant, but this will turn out to be very positive in the end. You are likely to have

Reversed

The Tower reversed is even more disruptive and chaotic. The firm you work for may collapse overnight, with loss of jobs all around. You could be sacked for totally unfair reasons, and find yourself unemployed and financially insecure. Again, negative as these changes appear on the surface there is a good reason behind them. It could take you some time to realize that you are now free to do something more interesting.

Similarly, relationships may break up very suddenly leaving you feeling vulnerable and puzzled. You want to know why, but the answer seems to lie hidden somewhere out of your reach.

Depending upon surrounding cards, the Tower reversed can also indicate some form of imprisonment. This can be literally interpreted, of course, but usually suggests that you are stuck in a negative situation where you cannot express yourself freely. You are unable to improve matters immediately, but this card promises that you will eventually achieve freedom – at a price.

17

THE STAR

SIGN: AQUARIUS

'The stars,
That nature hung in heaven,
    and filled their lamps
With everlasting oil, to give due light
To the misled and lonely traveller.'

Comus John Milton

Myths and symbols

The peaceful and beautiful image portrayed on the Star usually depicts a naked woman pouring water into a pool, and onto the land beside her. Seven stars shine in the sky above, while one larger star gleams in their midst.

The Pleiades, or Seven Sisters, is a constellation of seven stars which has been venerated by a number of cultures. The Ancient Greeks believed that they were the souls of seven maidens, or a flock of doves to which Aphrodite gave birth. The Romans referred to them as the 'Virgins of Spring', for they rise during May and herald the most fertile time of year.

Red Indian myths also refer to the Pleiades. The Dakota tribe say that these stars are the home of their ancestors, and that the spirits of the dead return there. The Iroquois address prayers for happiness to them, believing that the stars represent seven young people whose job it is to guard the holy seed during the night.

The larger star may be intended to represent fusion and transcendence. It is also said to refer to Ishtar, a powerful goddess who was worshipped for more than two thousand years in the Middle East. She is linked with Aphrodite, and presided over many things – including healing, eroticism, and agricultural prosperity.

The sign of Aquarius, the water-bearer, is the eleventh sign of the zodiac. Aquarius represents the blending of intuition – symbolized by water – and reason, symbolized by this sign's airy element. It is a sign associated with humanitarian ideals, inventiveness, and progressive thinking of every kind. The eleventh house traditionally denotes groups, societies, friendships, hopes and wishes – or ideals.

Seventeen, the number of the Star, was believed to be a very lucky number. Those born on the 17th were supposed to be intuitive, and destined to be wealthy. It was also said to be the number of immortality; beauty; self-expression and hope. Today, many people still like to 'wish upon a star', for it is an enduring symbol of hope.

Interpretation

The Star is a favourable and positive card. The old saying 'where there's life, there's hope' is particularly relevant to this image, for it signifies new life and renewed faith. When you draw this card in a reading you will be filled with hope. You gain fresh insight into an old problem, and are full of energy. Physical or mental wounds heal, vitality is restored, and your horizons open up.

You may be able to heal others, inspire them, or make them feel better about themselves in some way. If you are in need of such things, then the Star suggests that help will soon arrive from an unexpected direction.

Sometimes, the Star indicates a trip to the country or the need for more contact with nature. If you live in a city it is very easy to lose touch with the seasons, plants, birds and animals. These things can have a very healing influence on us, and the appearance of the Star indicates that much pleasure and joy can be gained from nature now.

When the Star relates to work, or personal interests, it usually refers to typically Aquarian concerns. These include human rights; equality of the sexes; all 'green' environmental issues; and organizations whose aim is to help others. You may find yourself involved with such movements on a practical level, or become increasingly concerned about them.

When this card refers to a relationship, it suggests a joyful and balanced partnership. A good sexual relationship is indicated; your needs are balanced and you make each other happy.

Reversed

Your bright hopes seem to have been dashed. You may feel depressed and pessimistic about the future, or doubt your own abilities. This mood could stem from actual events, or simply from exhaustion – you will know which it is if you think about it.

There is considerable tension in this position, and a stubborn refusal to let go. You may not be able to relax easily, and feel tired and generally fed up. The Star's message is still one of hope, however. The world will not cease to turn if you take a break.

In terms of a relationship, problems may come about through lack of trust in each other. Sexually, this can manifest as insecurity or difficulties with one's sexual identity. You, or your partner, may feel cut off, detached and unable to express love naturally and spontaneously. Again, tension and self–doubt may have a great deal to do with this obstacle.

Far left: The Star from the Marseilles deck (and **right:)** from the Waite deck

18

THE MOON

SIGN: PISCES

'She is the ruler of the tides of flux and reflux. The waters of the Great Sea answer unto her, likewise the tides of all earthly seas, and she ruleth the nature of woman.'

Dion Fortune

Myths and symbols

A full moon hangs in the sky over a surreal dream-like landscape. Two dogs tip back their heads and howl, while a crab crawls out of a pool. Two mysterious, and slightly sinister towers rise in the distance. This extraordinary and disquieting image is that of the Moon.

Symbolically, this picture has a number of interpretations. The crab or crayfish is said to represent our earliest stages of development. As we collectively crawl out of the pool of the unconscious, we become aware. Then we realize, perhaps, that there is more to the world than we had at first supposed. Spiritually and intellectually, we 'shoot for the moon'. The two towers represent the gateway through which we must pass if we want to attain enlightenment.

The presence of the moon and the two dogs also suggests links with numerous ancient myths. Many cultures believed that the souls of the dead journeyed to the moon, where they lived after death. The moon was also worshipped as the source of life and fertility, and was therefore usually – though not always – female. 'Drawing down the Moon' is a magical ritual still practised today to invoke the goddess, and call her down to temporarily inhabit a priestess.

Dogs, too, are often mythically linked with death and the moon. These creatures sometimes guarded the gates of death, or helped to carry the souls of the dead to the afterlife. Anubis, the ancient Egyptian god of the underworld, had the head of a jackal. And an old superstition states that when a dog howls at the moon it is an omen of death, for dogs are more sensitive than human beings and can see the Angel of Death approaching.

The Moon is assigned to Pisces, the twelfth sign of the natural zodiac. The two fishes, which symbolize the sign, swim in the deep waters of the unconscious. Pisces is associated with dreams, visions, imagination, creativity, intuition and unconditional love. Linked with the Moon, the message is one of transcending the physical and material.

Interpretation

The Moon has often been interpreted as a card of evil omen whether upright or reversed. The true meaning seems to have become lost, or bastardized, just as the true symbology behind moon worship remained hidden for centuries. Should you come across one of these frightening interpretations, try to ignore it – for it is based on superstition.

The Moon belongs to the world of dreams, psychic impressions, and imaginative ideas. If it appears in a position relating to yourself, you are entering a phase when your subconscious will be making itself felt. You may find yourself remembering peculiarly vivid dreams, full of symbols and messages.

You may become sharply aware of colour, drawn to visionary poetry, or immerse yourself in powerfully symbolic fiction. If you are a practical type, this may all be a little uncomfortable for it will feel as if you are losing control. Remember this is a watery card, and try to flow with these feelings yourself.

In career matters, the Moon relates to the world of illusion. This can manifest as theatre or film work; writing fiction or poetry; or translating personal visions into some kind of reality – a painting, play, interior or altruistic activity for example.

Sometimes this card refers to healing abilities or other psychic work. At others, it can indicate work in nightclubs or beautifully-decorated restaurants. An interest in, or work with psychology, the fields of dream-analysis and myths are other areas signified by the Moon.

Physically, the Moon sometimes suggests a need or longing for sleep. It can indicate water retention, menstrual problems, and the presence of toxins in the body. It is also linked with the lymph glands, which disperse such toxins and

Above: The Moon from the Marseilles deck

help to keep the skin clear. Massage, water-based therapies and reflexology (a form of stimulating pressure massage usually performed on the feet) are denoted by the Moon.

Reversed

The world of illusion can be positive or negative. Here we meet its darker face. You may be dealing with insincere people. You, or someone in your life, finds it hard to distinguish between fantasy and reality. Job offers or relationships falling may simply dissolve in the harsh light of reality. Keep your own counsel for hidden enemies may be working against you.

You may have to deal with alcoholism, drug abuse, depression, or people in prison or hospital when the Moon falls in the reversed position. Surrounding cards should provide further information on the subject.

19

THE SUN

PLANET: SUN

'Thy dawning is beautiful in the horizon of
heaven,
Oh living Aton, beginning of life.
When thou risest in the eastern horizon
of heaven,
Though fillest every land with thy beauty;
For thou art beautiful, great, glittering,
high over the earth;
Thy rays they encompass the lands, even
all thou hast made.
Thou art Ra and thou hast carried them all
away captive;
Thou bindest them by thy love.
Though thou art afar thy rays are on the
earth;
Though thou art on high thy footprints are
the day.'

Egyptian Hymn to the Sun
Akhenaton, alias Amenhotep IV

Above left: The Sun from the
Marseilles deck (and **right:**) from the Waite deck

Myths and symbols

The Sun follows the Moon in the Tarot,
just as sun-ruled Leo follows moon-
ruled Cancer in the zodiac. This great
burning star symbolizes the bright
forces of energy, vitality, joy and glory.

Apollo was the Greek god of the Sun,
while his twin sister Artemis was the
Moon goddess. A powerful and popular
figure, he was god of prophecy, music,
healing, and archery. He was also often
linked with the female muses, and
shared patronage of the arts of poetry,
dancing and music with them in many
myths. He is usually shown as a beautiful
young man at the height of his powers,
radiant and virile. Ancient Egyptians
venerated the sun as Re or Ra; he was
closely connected with the pharoahs
who were believed to represent the
deity on earth.

In astrology, the sun governs Leo, and
the fifth house of the zodiac, associated
with creativity, self-expression, games,
pleasures and romance. Children – of
the mind or body – are also linked to
the sun's house. A child, or two children are usually shown on this card.
Interpretations are that the children
have emerged from the womb represented by the Moon into the full light of
consciousness; a union between the
hidden, subconscious aspects of the

personality and the clarity of intellectual expression has been achieved.

In many mythologies the sun and moon were twins, symbolizing two halves of a whole; light and dark, positive and negative, intellect and intuition. The children also represent innocence, joy, and new creations. Some commentators say that the Sun represents the higher self.

Interpretation

Happiness and vitality are entering your life. You could find yourself better off financially; enjoy your work or experience a particularly joyful time in your relationship. Socially, you are invited to events where you can bask in the warmth of friendship, and enjoy yourself.

When this card refers to yourself, its message is one of energy and confidence. You are glowing with good health, able to achieve your dreams. If you have been struggling things will get easier now. Your mind feels clear, and you are able to make far-sighted plans. Life is good, there is nothing to worry about for success is certain.

The Sun can also manifest literally in a reading. It can signify summer, or refer to hot, sunny climates. Summer may be an important time of year for you, a time when things go well and you are able to celebrate some success or happy event. A hot country could be significant in terms of fortunate meetings, the beginning of a new career, or a wonderful holiday. Look to surrounding cards to see whether a particular aspect has been emphasized elsewhere.

Children are also represented by this card. There may be good news regarding them. A child develops a natural talent; a longed-for baby is born; a child who has been ill or in difficulties wins through.

Reversed

The sun's warmth is essential for life. Yet an excess of heat creates deserts and destroys living things. When you draw the Sun reversed, you may expect a failure of some kind. Doubts surround your future plans. Vanity and arrogance are indicated as probable blocks to success.

In terms of a relationship, you may be experiencing difficulties. This is particularly true if you are married, or living with an established partner. You may feel taken for granted, unappreciated or feel you are not getting enough attention. Other cards should indicate both background and solutions to this problem.

Similar difficulties may be pervading a business partnership. Both partners may not see eye to eye, or one feels he or she is putting in more than the other. Perhaps one wants to initiate new activities, while the other is resisting change.

There may be worries concerning children. Hyperactive babies and children may be exhausting and puzzling their parents. A child could be oversensitive either physically – allergies – or mentally. There might be problems at school, too.

Finally, if the Sun reversed is surrounded by positive, upright cards you can expect happiness and success but it will be delayed.

20

JUDGMENT

PLANET: PLUTO

'At the round earth's imagined corners,
  blow
Your trumpets, Angels, and arise, arise
From death, your numberless infinities
Of souls.'

Holy Sonnets, VII John Donne

Myths and symbols

Judgment, like some of the other Tarot images, seems to fit nicely into the medieval world. It is a familiar Christian image: the great archangel Michael blows his horn, sounds the Last Trump, and the souls of the dead rise up at his call.

This idea of the last days of the world is not unique to Christianity, for it is found in many ancient cultures, including Hindu, Norse, Persian and Ancient Roman mythology. Some kind of rebirth, new creation, or resurrection follows the dreadful destruction – and is usually announced by signs and portents beforehand.

Pluto, Lord of the Underworld, has been attached to this card since the planet's discovery earlier this century. This planet, now joint ruler of Scorpio with Mars, represents the forces of transformation in astrology. But these dark energies are rarely comfortable, or easy to handle. Frequently the destruction of old habits or outworn concepts precedes the transformation promised by Pluto's influence. Pluto, as god of the dark places beneath the earth, was often said to preside over buried treasure and valuable jewels. Such riches are not easily found, but when they are they bring great rewards to their possessor.

Many esoteric cults used the idea of death and rebirth, which is also suggested by this card. Initiates would undergo frightening and solemn rituals as part of their training; many of these included spending time alone in a dark place. They then would be symbolically 'reborn', and enter the light once more. Judgment is followed by the World, which is the true last trump of the Tarot, symbolizing completion and fulfilment of the highest kind.

Interpretation

Sometimes Judgment makes itself felt in a literal way, for it can signify decisions. Such decisions are usually pressing, and must be made if your life is to improve. If you were worried about making such a decision when you consulted the cards, you may rest assured that it will have a positive outcome.

Judgment can also indicate an awakening. Perhaps you have been working in the dark, and can now see things more clearly. You feel restored and renewed mentally, physically or emotionally – often all three. With this new and vital energy at your disposal you are able to enjoy and appreciate your partner, friends, family and work.

Above: Judgment from the Marseilles deck

This is a very positive card to draw if you are concerned about your health, or that of someone else. It indicates that healing has taken place, convalescence is over, and the person is back on his or her feet.

In terms of career, it suggests that you are free to enjoy your work and celebrate your successes. Should you be considering a change of career, Judgment signifies that this would be an excellent move to make. Whether change, promotion, or retirement lies ahead you have reached the end of a cycle. But something interesting and stimulating follows; if any cards fall after Judgment these should throw some light on what it may be.

Reversed

For some reason a decision which needs to be made is being delayed. This is creating a stagnant pause in your life, and preventing much happening. If you are dithering about something now is the time to make up your mind once and for all. If you delay you may lose something or someone of value to you.

Traditionally, Judgment reversed signifies fear of death. Death can take many forms, and on one level represents major changes. So this position can also mean fear of change – another reason for delaying decisions and sitting on the fence.

Emotionally, this position denotes a loss of some kind. You and your partner may have to spend some time apart, but the break is not necessarily final. One of you may even have to go away because of work, and be forcibly separated for a time. If things have been going badly in your relationship, it may indeed be drawing to an end but neither of you is able to say 'good-bye' just yet.

Above: Judgment from the Waite deck

21
THE WORLD
♄

PLANET: SATURN

'Dance then wherever you may be
I am the Lord of the Dance, said he,
And I'll lead you all, wherever you may be,
And I'll lead you all in the dance, said he.'

Sydney Carter

Above: The World from the Waite deck

Myths and symbols

The cycle ushered in by the Fool is completed, the next spiral turn awaits. The World is usually depicted as a naked woman dancing inside an oval wreath. Each of the four corners shows one of the archetypal creatures also seen on the Wheel of Fortune. Indeed, this card was sometimes known as the Major Fortune.

Here is balance, symbolized by the four elements – Fire, Earth, Air and Water. The lessons and experiences represented by the Major Arcana have all been synthesized, absorbed and completion has been achieved.

The oval wreath resembles an egg. The Cosmic Egg is an ancient symbol of wholeness, knowledge and wisdom. Within this shape the joyful dancing figure suggests that the dance of life continues in a never–ending cycle of birth and death.

Some experts maintain that the dancing figure is an hermaphrodite, for these rare creatures denote a perfect blending of our male and female qualities. Others say that the figure is definitely a woman who symbolizes the Great Goddess, creatress of life and mother of all the gods.

The World is associated with the planet Saturn. This planet was known as Rex Mundi, Lord of the World, to ancient astrologers. Saturn is the planet of structure, boundaries, self-discipline and the limitations of matter. The limitations of the physical world must be come to terms with if spiritual progress is to be made. Without Saturn nothing would ever be achieved, or brought into material reality.

Saturn was known as Kronos to the Greeks, and Geb, god of earth to the Egyptians. Both these gods governed time – another of life's inevitable limitations. The dual symbolic message of this card seems to be that spirit must penetrate matter in order to evolve.

Above: Magician; a 19th-century mezzotint of a conjuring magician

Below: Hierophant; bull-leaping fresco from Knossos, c.1600 BC Minoan palace, Crete

Left: Lovers; lovers in an 18th-century miniature from Rajasthan

Below: Hermit; a 17th-century picture of a hermit, with the alchemist Sendovius to the left, signalling inner transformation

Above: Justice; an Egyptian image of Justice, from a papyrus of about 1250 BC, showing a soul being weighed in the scales of Justice by the Jackal-headed god Anubis

Above: Wheel of Fortune; the Wheel of Fortune, from the 15th-century Flemish *Roman de la Rose* manuscript

Right: Hanged Man; Yggdrasill, the Tree of Life of Norse myth

Below: Tower; Brueghel's Tower of Babel

Left: Star; Hope personified by G.F. Watts

Below: Judgment; a late Byzantine fresco of the Day of Judgment, from St Saviour in Chora, Istanbul

Left: World; the world snake, from a 17th-century alchemical work

Below: Fool; clowns engraved by the Dutch artist Cock, after a design by Brueghel

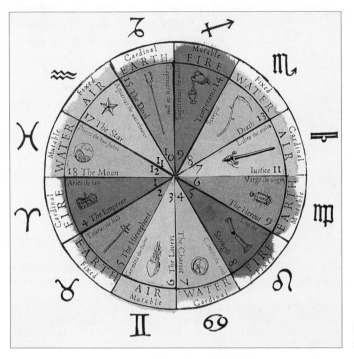

Left: The Major Arcana and the zodiac

Right: The Major Arcana and the planets

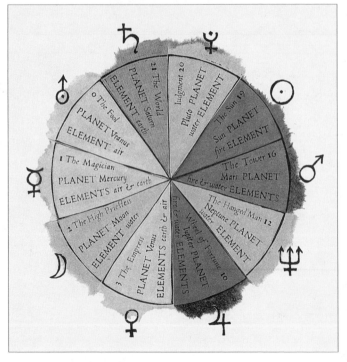

Interpretation

You have reached the end of a cycle in your life, there is a sense of completion and accomplishment. This influence may appear on many levels. You may have finished an important project at work; a creative endeavour of your own; or a long-term course of education. You may have successfully integrated some previously-dormant aspect of your personality and become a more fully-rounded person.

The World signifies success and fulfilment, whatever your question may have been. So although a cycle is ending, and a door is closing, it is also a time for celebration. Perhaps you are starting a family, and leaving behind the single life. Older people may find that their children are leaving home and should welcome the potential freedom this represents.

If your question referred to career, you will be delighted with the outcome. A new job or promotion will be everything you hoped for, and you will not want to go back to how things were before. Sometimes this card can even foretell fame, public acclaim and attention – especially in the arts. Enjoy your achievements, and the temporary pinnacle they represent. The World is the last trump, and as it turns the Fool reappears and a fresh cycle begins.

In terms of a relationship, you may look forward to balance and happiness. Perhaps a difficult or testing time is now over, and you can both enjoy the insights this has brought. You are now free to bring out the best in each other,

and enjoy the differences between you.

The World may also manifest as a journey, new home, or new place of work. You are literally being given a chance to see more of the world we live in. Journeys signified by this card will inspire you, expand your knowledge, and bring insight and happiness. When the World refers to a new home, or other change of environment, it denotes a change for the better. Your old home or job has served its purpose well; now you are ready to move on.

Reversed

Completion is still implied, but it has been delayed. You may find this frustrating, and want to speed things up in some way but cannot see how. Or you do not want something to reach its conclusion; like a child reading a wonderful book you don't want to get to the last page. But you cannot avoid this forever, and must let go. The World reversed implies a resistance to change in some shape or form.

If your question referred to a relationship, there is some unfinished business between you. Perhaps you are blocking a potential partner because you are tied to the past in some way. Perhaps a fear of being hurt is causing the hesitation. Try to come to terms with your past, and realize that living in its shadows may be preventing future happiness. Open your heart, there is nothing to fear – the World is telling you that a positive relationship lies ahead.

If you draw this card when asking

about your work you may be ill-prepared in some way, or feel you are. You do not know the words for your speech; the paint has not dried on the canvas; the house is upside-down and you are expecting visitors. Or you may think something is finished – it isn't.

There is something else that needs to be done before completion may be finalized. However, the World is a positive card upright or reversed. It signifies natural changes, which are invariably welcome once you have come to terms with their inevitability.

THE MINOR ARCANA

*While the Major Arcana embodies large, universal concepts, the
Minor Arcana weaves amongst them, filling in the details. These
fifty-six cards relate to everyday existence; passing thoughts, events
and feelings – and the people who contribute to the pattern of our
lives. This does not make them any less important than the Major
Arcana – just easier to deal with and understand.*

◆ ◆ ◆

Laying the cards without using the Minor Arcana can give a very distorted view of things. After all, life is rarely filled with dramatic and memorable events on a weekly basis. These cards are important, for they often reveal the apparently inconsequential threads which will eventually form a meaningful pattern. They can also show you how the influence of a major card will manifest itself in normal life.

To give a simplified example: if you drew the High Priestess in a reading she could indicate many things, including secrets, psychic work, or a mysterious woman. The minor cards around her might suggest that this particular energy would be found in working life (the suit of Pentacles); love life (the suit of Cups); or represent new ways of thinking (the suit of Swords).

Elementary elements

Each suit of the Minor Arcana symbol-izes one of the four elements. Cups belong to the element of water; Wands represent fire; Swords signify air; and Pentacles, earth.

These four elements were regarded by ancient philosophers as the building blocks of the universe. Consequently, they are found in many guises including the Four Humours of early medicine; in astrology; and as the four quarters of the traditional magic circle. There is a fifth element, ether, which symbolizes transcendence and the world of spirit. This is represented in the Minor Arcana by the tens.

Jung and the elements

Carl Jung proposed the idea of four basic personality functions, one of which tends to dominate, while the others require effort to develop if we are to become whole. He said, 'For complete orientation all four functions should contribute equally.'

Jung's functions can be usefully linked to the four elements, their astrological signs, and relevant Tarot suit, as shown in the chart below.

Jung's personality functions linked to the elements, the Tarot and the Sun Signs.			
FUNCTION	ELEMENT	TAROT SUIT	SUN SIGNS
Intuition	Fire	Wands	Aries, Leo, Sagittarius
Sensation	Earth	Pentacles	Taurus, Virgo, Capricorn
Thinking	Air	Swords	Gemini, Libra, Aquarius
Feeling	Water	Cups	Cancer, Scorpio, Pisces

Each element can be seen as a particular type of energy. An understanding, and knowledge of its attributes can help spark off your intuition when you are reading the cards.

By exploring the fascinating web of elemental meanings and correspondences you can begin to grasp the 'flavour' of the four suits. In this way you are less likely to get lost amidst their individual meanings. Each element seems to conjure up a mood, and each has its special place on the wheel of life.

Right: 15th century Tarot cards from Florence showing an astrologer and the 12 signs of the zodiac

ASTROLOGY AND THE MINOR ARCANA

The Minor Arcana has been usefully coupled with astrology, both through the four elements and the twelve signs of the zodiac. This partnership provides numerous correspondences, cross-links and amplified meanings. A basic working knowledge of signs and planets can help bring the minor cards to life, or suggest fresh angles in a reading. If you are completely unfamiliar with astrology, it is advisable to wait until you have a good grasp of the Tarot before exploring these parallels.

Using astrology with the court cards

The astrological meanings attached to the court cards are also helpful when you want to choose a significator for a spread, or clearly identify an important character in a reading.

For example, by asking what sign your querent was born under – or looking it up in the list of dates of the Zodiac signs below, you can swiftly choose an appropriate card. With a birthday falling on the 6th of May, for instance, he or she would be a Taurean, and so you would pick the King or Queen of Pentacles to represent the person in your spread.

Sometimes, situations involve a choice between two potential business partners or lovers. In business, you are unlikely to be able to find out the individuals' birthsigns – but as long as the two characters are sufficiently different you should be able to separate them using the astrological character-sketches, methods of working, and ways of thinking.

In love, birthsigns (or at least birthdays) are likely to be known. You can then see whether the cards reveal two signs, and whether these correspond to the people involved. Where there are two men or women of the same sign, look for a King and a Knight of the same suit, or a Queen and a Page of the same suit. To clarify matters, it is a good idea to do a separate spread for each person, choosing an astrologically suitable card to represent them.

The signs of the zodiac, with their dates

ARIES the Ram: 21st March – 20th April
TAURUS the Bull: 21st April – 20th May
GEMINI the Twins 21st May – 21st June
CANCER the Crab: 22nd June – 23rd July
LEO the Lion: 23rd July – 22nd August
VIRGO the Virgin: 23rd August – 22nd September
LIBRA the Scales: 23rd September – 23rd October
SCORPIO the Scorpion: 24th October – 21st November
SAGITTARIUS the Archer: 22nd November – 21st December
CAPRICORN the Goat: 22nd December – 19th January
AQUARIUS the Water–Bearer: 20th January – 18th February
PISCES the Fishes: 19th February – 20th March.

ASTROLOGICAL CORRESPONDENCES AND THE MINOR ARCANA

Astrology teaches that each elemental group of signs may be divided into three; Cardinal, Fixed, and Mutable. These groups are called the triplicities. The cardinal signs of each group initiate things. The four cardinal signs are Aries, Cancer, Libra and Capricorn and correspond in Tarot to the Aces, twos and threes of their particular suit. The fixed signs of the zodiac are Taurus, Leo, Scorpio and Aquarius. They consolidate matters, and correspond to the fours, fives, and sixes of their particular suit. The mutable signs are Gemini, Virgo, Sagittarius and Pisces. They are changeable in nature and correspond to the sevens, eights and nines of their suit.

The four tens sum up the energies, and seem to intensify the meaning of their ruling element. They are linked with the symbolic fifth element, spirit or ether, and are not linked with any individual astrological signs.

Each sign of the zodiac has a ruling planet. These planets were traditionally associated with a wide range of things, such as plants, foods, colours, animals, and birds. These links are known as 'correspondences', and symbolize how the energy of each planet can manifest itself in varied, but connected ways.

Correspondences can help stimulate your imagination when reading the cards; they act as a jumping-off point – especially when you are feeling 'stuck', or are finding it hard to make sense of a spread. Here is a small selection which you may find helpful.

THE ELEMENT OF FIRE
THE SUIT OF WANDS
ARIES, LEO AND SAGITTARIUS

SIGN: ARIES   PLANET: MARS

The Ace, two, and three of Wands

Colour: Vivid, glowing scarlet.
Career clues: The innovator, boss, leader, authority figure.
Typical places: Crowded bars; noisy parties; bright busy places.
Love phases: Passionate, speedy, argumentative affairs.

SIGN: LEO   PLANET: SUN

The four, five and six of Wands

Colour: Warm golden hues.
Career clues: Creative jobs; public relations; lecturing; the theatre.

Typical places: Expensive, lavishly-decorated hotels and restaurants; palaces; mountainous regions; theatres and places of entertainment.
Love phases: Romantic, playful relationships or interludes.

SIGN: SAGITTARIUS   PLANET: JUPITER

The seven, eight and nine of Wands

Colour: Purple, deep sapphire blue.
Career clues: Those who travel in their work; explorers; salesmen; the self-employed.
Typical places: Stations; airports; hillsides; stables; wide open spaces.
Love phases: Friendship first, love second, and personal freedom above all.

THE ELEMENT OF EARTH
THE SUIT OF PENTACLES
TAURUS, VIRGO, CAPRICORN

SIGN: CAPRICORN   PLANET: SATURN

The Ace, two and three of Pentacles

Colour: Deep, earthy brown; granite grey.
Career clues: Self-disciplined work; property and land connections; sensible planning; solid structures of every kind from bricks and mortar to a well-thought-out contract.
Typical places: Beautiful old buildings; traditional, old-fashioned hotels; harbours; places where quality triumphs over passing trends.
Love phases: Rock-steady, committed, conventional.

SIGN: TAURUS   PLANET: VENUS

Four, five and six of Pentacles

Colour: Rich, vibrant bluey green.
Career clues: Tending and nurturing projects; being resourceful; practical creativity.
Typical places: Herb and vegetable gardens; orchards, especially apple orchards; comfortable, sometimes luxurious, environments.
Love phases: Sensuous, indulgent, possessive.

Sign: Virgo Planet: Mercury

The seven, eight and nine of Pentacles

Colour: Grey and navy
Career clues: Those who work behind the scenes; service industries; hospital or other health work; cleaners and statisticians.
Typical places: Health-food restaurants; doctor's surgeries; the countryside; corn fields.
Love phases: Needing to be needed; criticizing someone 'for their own good'; selfless love.

THE ELEMENT OF AIR
THE SUIT OF SWORDS
GEMINI, LIBRA AND AQUARIUS

Sign: Gemini Planet: Mercury

The seven, eight and nine of Swords

Colour: Bi-coloured things; yellow; light grey.
Career clues: Telephone conversations are highlighted; publishing; media; agents; writers; interpreters; musicians.
Typical places: Aeroplanes; open-plan offices; universities; libraries.
Love phases: Talking till dawn; two-timing; flirtation without commitment.

Sign: Libra Planet: Venus

The Ace, two and three of Swords

Colour: Sky blue.
Career clues: Lawyers; beauticians; hairdressers; mediators of all kinds; those whose iron fist is concealed in an elegant velvet glove.
Typical places: Rose-gardens; peaceful, tasteful places; bedrooms; luxurious beauty parlours.
Love phases: Detached, chilly moments; indecisive lovers; sentimental phases.

Sign: Aquarius Planet: Uranus / Saturn

Four, five and six of Swords

Colour: Electric blue.
Career clues: Working in new fields, or with revolutionary ideas; electronics; broadcasting; work pertaining to the mass of humanity such as charities; social movements; progressive organizations.
Typical places: Unusual locations; strangely-decorated places; anywhere where groups meet.
Love phases: Sudden attractions; unconventional relationships.

THE ELEMENT OF WATER
THE SUIT OF CUPS
CANCER, SCORPIO, PISCES

Sign: Cancer Planet: Moon

The Ace, two and three of Cups

Colour: Misty pastels, silver.
Career clues: Occupations connected with women; caring for people, animals, plants; catering for others; nourishing or protecting a business, creative idea, team or project.
Typical places: Kitchens; places with a view of water; boats; charming, old-fashioned environments filled with antiques.
Love phases: Domestic happiness; heightened emotions; moody moments.

Sign: Scorpio Planet: Mars / Pluto

The four, five and six of Cups

Colour: Deep, jewel-like reds and blues; black.
Career clues: Research and detective work of every kind; recycling ideas or substances; secretive projects.
Typical places: Basements and cellars; near water; vineyards; quiet, dimly-lit environments.
Love phases: Repressed or passionate sex; death and rebirth in relationships; jealousy.

Sign: Pisces Planet: Jupiter / Neptune

The seven, eight and nine of Cups

Colour: All the colours of the oceans.
Career clues: Creating beautiful illusions, art, films, 'images'; therapeutic work; confusion; visionary ideas.
Typical places: Exotic, mysterious environments, untidy muddles; swimming pools; the sea.
Love phases: Devoted, self-sacrificing love; pain and loss; romantic illusions; elusive relationships.

THE MINOR ARCANA AND THE ELEMENTS

Linking Up

Moving from the centre of the wheel outwards, this illustration relates the 12 signs of the zodiac to Jung's four basic personality functions – described on page 68 – to the four suits of the Minor Arcana, and to the seasons and elements that correspond to each. The links are made for you to refer to at your leisure and pleasure; it is not necessary to set out to memorize them. The text in this introductory section to the Minor Arcana is here to amplify the descriptions of each card, which follow on pages 81–135. Weaving in and out of one another, any of these correspondences may just serve to trigger off some fresh insight when you are examining or reading the Tarot cards.

Expanding awareness

For example, you may be conscious that the earth signs of the zodiac – Taurus, Virgo and Capricorn – denote practical people who like to have a high degree of material luxury in their lives, but the additional association with Jung's personality function of sensation may give a further dimension to your understanding of this type of personality.

THE ELEMENT OF FIRE THE SUIT OF WANDS

Season: Summer
Elemental Spirit: Salamander

Jungian Function: Intuitive
Keywords: Inception / Energy / Heat / Illumination / Vision / Action

The volatile, vital energy of fire is expressed through the suit of Wands. Fire corresponds to Jung's intuitive type. It is the force behind the sudden inspirations of the artist, mystic, entrepreneur, or charismatic leader. The ability to see – both mentally and physically – is associated with fire. Wands relate to the inner eye of the creative thinker, who may bring his or her talents to business, politics, or the arts.

This element is also closely linked to the symbolic worlds of myths, legends and fairy-tales. There is something larger-than-life about it, and it may represent drama in personal life or mental attitudes. Fire's beautiful pictures and images inspire others, but can easily be lost or forgotten if something is not done about them quickly. Fiery emotions, too, may flare up suddenly and just as swiftly die down.

Boredom, routine, and lack of vision or enthusiasm can all extinguish fire's vital energy. A lone Wand, for example, may lose much of its force when surrounded by negative watery Cups. Fire can also be destructive and impractical on occasion, so always look carefully at the Wands to see how they are placed before assuming they are active and positive.

But basically, Fire represents optimism – the triumph of hope over experience. Even when this optimism is misplaced, it somehow usually wins through. There is a clue to be found in the traditional magical imagery linked with this element: the clear shining light of the noonday sun casts few shadows, and chases away doubt and confusion.

When Wands predominate in a spread they bring energy, movement, optimism and creativity. They are associated with travel, and can signify interesting trips for business or pleasure. Wands can also denote mental travelling. Inner journeys, filled with mental challenges, are typically suggested by this suit.

Traditionally, Wands also indicate deals and negotiations; your career in the broadest sense; property matters; and sparkling gatherings such as parties, and lively social events.

The court cards and the element of fire

Wands relate to the three fire signs of the zodiac: Aries, Leo and Sagittarius. When court cards appear in a spread, they frequently indicate a person, and sometimes stand for a state of mind or situation.

When you get the King, Queen, Knight or Page of Wands in a spread they usually appear as a fiery type. The person denoted may actually be a fire sign, fire signs could dominate his or her horoscope, or 'fiery' behaviour may be characteristic.

It is important to realize that a thumbnail sketch of each sign can only suggest the broadest possible character traits. Real-life human beings are much more complex and subtle. However, these traits can prove helpful in a reading by giving you a handy, if superficial, idea of the type of person who may be playing a part in your life.

Fiery people and situations are characterized by drama, idealism, vision and exuberance. When the Wands appear in an upright position they signify the inspirational strength and extrovert qualities of fire. When you are unable to pinpoint the exact type, it is safe to assume that the people represented by Wands are active, extrovert, dramatic and charmingly selfish.

Each of the three fire signs is primarily concerned with self-expression. Aries, the Ram, takes risks in order to achieve success. Ariens are the great initiators of the zodiac, impatient, impulsive and pioneering. When Wands represent these types, they are often playing a leading role in your life – particularly in business, or encouraging your own fiery qualities. They bring energy and urgency with them, and often spark off bright ideas.

Leo, the Lion, evinces the qualities of loyalty, creativity, and trust. These types are often very romantic, idealistic, and generous. They can inspire others with their fiery energy and warmth of expression. When Wands represent Leonine people, they tend to stress the glamorous, golden side of this sun sign.

Those who work in the theatre, entertainment business or other media may be represented by Wands. In relationships, Leo Wands represent warm, romantic types who still require quite a lot of personal space. They may be unfairly possessive of others while guarding their own freedom – it is one rule for them, and another for everyone else.

Sagittarius, the Archer, is expansive, honest and extraordinarily optimistic. Sagittarians are traditionally the spiritual and temporal philosophers of the zodiac, for their eyes are always focused upon the far horizons.

When the Wands symbolize these qualities, they usually stand for travellers, foreign business contacts, or sometimes elusive and colourful figures who are impossible to pin down. Thus, they can stand for friends who brighten your life temporarily, ebullient colleagues, or unreliable lovers.

Ariens can be totally selfish and insensitive to others. They may fly into destructive rages, or become bored and detached. In their desire to lead, to win, to do, they may trample heedlessly over less stalwart souls. When the Wands represent the negative face of Aries, they usually appear in a work context.

Leo's vanity, need for attention, and overwhelming sense of drama can edge all the other players off the stage. Everything must centre on Leos, and if it doesn't they will sulk, or create theatrical scenes. These negative Wand traits usually appear within a close relationship, indicating the kind of problems which are surfacing.

Sagittarians' idealism can turn into unrealized dreams, which they are too slapdash to ground in reality. They may waste their talents, or scatter their considerable energy to the four winds. When the Wands denote these tendencies, they may be found in the context of career, life-patterns, and sometimes personal relationships.

THE ELEMENT OF EARTH
THE SUIT OF PENTACLES

Season: Winter
Elemental Spirit: Gnome – and not the garden variety!
Jungian Function: Sensation
Keywords: Practical / Supportive / Patient / Grounded / Realistic / Structured

The element of earth is expressed through the suit of Pentacles. It represents the material world – everything we can see, taste, smell and touch. Earth and the Pentacles symbolize old-fashioned common sense, the ability to toil away until something has been achieved, commitment and practicality.

This suit denotes real money, bricks and mortar, and hard work. Fiery visions, exciting airy ideas, and water's inarticulate emotions all need a container if they are to become tangible. Earth, and the suit of Pentacles, represent that firm structure.

Pentacles is an important suit to look for in a reading because it stands for this kind of objective reality. Career plans, dream homes, financial hopes and emotional longings may all remain in the realm of the possible without a little earthy practicality to solidify them.

Earth, by its very nature, supports us. It denotes the foundations and limitations of life, which are ultimately inescapable. This may sound very dreary, especially if you yourself are an imaginative, free spirit. But without the qualities evinced by earth, there would be no aeroplanes to waft us away on escapist holidays, no houses to live in – indeed, there would be no physical reality at all.

And this sensual element has a magic of its own. It represents our sense of touch, without which it would be very difficult to express love, or create works of art. In magical imagery, earth can be visualized as a still, starlit winter's night filled with the scent of pine-trees and the promise of snow.

Earth stands for the wisdom of old age; supportive maternal instincts; and all actions which seek to preserve and consolidate. Pentacles bring these qualities into a reading, denoting money; work – as opposed to career; property; status and worldly matters in general.

The court cards and the element of earth

The suit of Pentacles is linked with the earth signs of Taurus, Virgo and Capricorn. The court cards of this suit represent people who demonstrate earthy traits in themselves, or are playing this role in your life.

Broadly speakihg, the earth signs and their court cards stand for practical people who are often well-off, work hard, and require routine in their lives. They are also warm, sensual, and fond of material comforts. In relationships they prefer commitment to flirtation, and may lack a sense of humour or imagination when it comes to others' failings.

Pentacle people can also be extremely supportive in useful, practical ways. They may find it difficult to sympathize with you over the phone, but will readily lend money, cook meals, or organize help when you need it. They are frequently good with their hands, too. Marvellous in a crisis, they are also excellent hosts and lasting friends.

When representing negative traits, Pentacles denote obstinacy, a stick-in-the-mud attitude, and often greed and materialism. Lack of vision, and authoritarian attitudes can also be suggested.

Taurus, the Bull, is loving, loyal and enjoys the good things of life. When the court cards represent this sign they tend to focus on these expansive earthy qualities. Taurean Pentacles are usually good cooks, and love large meals – accompanied by generous glasses of wine.

They are in tune with the earth, making excellent gardeners who are not afraid to get mud beneath their fingernails. Their fixed sense of loyalty is not given lightly, and the same is required of friends and lovers.

When Pentacles express negative Taurean characteristics, they point to stubborn individuals who will not listen to reason. There may be jealousy, or a wilful inability to understand a situation or point of view. Commitment to a relationship or business may be required by these people before others are ready to take this step. Conflict is the result.

Virgo, the Virgin, represents the lightest of the three earth signs. The Virgoan qualities of order, delicacy, and service to others can be denoted by the court cards – particularly when the spread refers to work or health matters. Medical people can be represented by the King, Queen, and Knight of Pentacles, as are those whose work involves creating order, or providing valuable back-up services behind the scenes. When negative, Virgoan Pentacle people represent critics, hypochondriacs, and those who cannot see the wood for the trees.

Capricorn, the Goat, can be cold and exceedingly dry. But beneath a forbidding exterior lies a steadfast and loving heart.

When the Pentacles denote the qualities of this sign they may appear as someone in authority – your boss, parents, or head of an organization.

They may also represent someone older than you – mentally, or chronologically. The apparent severity of these people masks their strength, patience,

and amazing stamina. When negative, Capricorn Pentacles can suggest rigidity, meanness and pessimism.

THE ELEMENT OF AIR
THE SUIT OF SWORDS

Season: Spring
Elemental Spirit: Sylph
Jungian Function: Thinking
Keywords: Thought / Logic / Reason / Intellect / Questioning / Light

The element of air symbolizes the plane of thought, and all structured mental activity. When positive, it is bright and breezy, and only touches the earth lightly – if at all. Symbolically, air corresponds to a spring dawn; a light breeze swirls through the trees, the air is clear, the day is just beginning.

Air, and the Swords, are linked with the so-called civilized mind. Here, ideas are carefully thought-out, analysed and labelled. Incisive questions, word games, written and spoken communications are all airy.

This fresh, light element brings reason and – on occasion – balance to the suit of Swords. At their best, Swords can represent great mental power and clarity. They are connected with the law, mathematics, and science. They may relate to mental and physical travel, new ideas, transforming thoughts. Yet this suit has a bad reputation. Cards of ill omen seem to abound, foretelling ruin, arguments, instability and disharmony of every kind. It is difficult to see where such an unfortunate interpretation arose, or why one suit should be considered so unlucky.

Above: The planet Venus, associated with romance and luxury rules the earth and the air signs, Taurus and Libra, as shown in this 15th century manuscript

The swords are indeed difficult cards on the whole, but they often refer to abstract situations or mental states rather than tangible actions or events. Words, communications, conversations and verbal arguments are frequent themes.

Traditionally, it is the dark and chaotic face of this element which manifests through the Swords. The power of negative thinking to cause unhappiness is often underestimated. When the qualities symbolized by air fail to connect with feeling, intuition or practicality, they can create a chilly, remote and inhuman world.

In this imaginary world the intellect rules, logic is all, and there is no room for mystery and imagination. Because it is fundamentally sterile, it is ultimately depressing and life-denying. This is the negative message of the Swords.

Their positive message is often undervalued. Swords can herald great mental changes, spark off our desire to learn, to read, and to explore ideas. Mental change is often the hardest of all, which may be why there is so much suffering represented by this suit.

The court cards and the element of air

The signs of the zodiac linked with Swords are Gemini, Libra and Aquarius. These airy signs, expressed through the court cards, represent thinkers and intellectuals. People symbolized by the suit of Swords are usually communicative, fair-.minded, and may be progressive thinkers. They are fascinated by

information, and the organization of ideas into a coherent whole.

Emotionally, they may appear cold and aloof on the surface, or fickle and insubstantial. They do have very deep feelings, but have tremendous difficulty in expressing them or even admitting to them. Swords often represent educated, professional types such as lawyers, scientists, architects and all those with sharp, quick minds.

When negative, Swords represent people who are malicious, spiteful and verbally aggressive. Their pens and tongues are certainly great weapons, for they rarely resort to physical violence – preferring to wound with words. They may also represent liars, and those who steal ideas.

Gemini, the Twins, is expressed through Swords as lively, talkative individuals. Such people may appear in your social life; their sparkling wit and wide-ranging conversation can be delightful. People who enjoy playing with words, writers, broadcasters, and public speakers are also represented here. When negative, Gemnian Swords may manifest as liars, smooth-talking conmen, and unfaithful partners, their quicksilver changeability can be exhausting, and they scatter their talents to the four winds.

Libra, the Scales, brings the idea of balance and fairness, law and order. Libran Swords are often lawyers or negotiators of some kind concerned with establishing equality, and injecting a note of reason into heated disagreements.

Negatively, Libran Swords manifest as

cold, power-hungry types or dithering advice-seekers. Either way, they are extremely selfish and rarely spare a thought for others.

Aquarius, the Waterbearer, manifests through the Swords as idealistic, inventive thinkers and eccentrics. Those who are attracted to progressive movements, politics, and visionary spiritual philosophies can be represented by Aquarian Swords. These types are often attached to a group and are concerned about the fate of humanity.

When negative, Aquarian Swords appear as people who find one-to-one relationships extremely difficult. It is easy for them to care about the planet, but very hard for them to give their full attention to an emotional relationship. Obstinate reformers are also represented by negative Swords, who think their way is the only way.

Above: The moon, planetary ruler of Cancer, straddles Cancer's symbol the Crab.

THE ELEMENT OF WATER
THE SUIT OF CUPS

Season: Autumn
Elemental Spirit: Undines
Jungian Function: Feeling
Keywords: Receptive / Loving / Flowing / Cleansing / Nurturing / Fulfilment

The element of water symbolizes the world of emotion, and corresponds to Jung's Feeling type. Water is essential if relationships, creativity, and group endeavours are to flourish and grow, for it represents the ability to nurture life.

Like its ruling element, the suit of Cups brings sensitivity and emotion into a reading, Cups relate to love, mar-riage, romance, and close relationships of every kind.

The depth of feeling suggested by this suit and its element flows into many areas. It can emerge as a sense of creativity, abundant ideas, and artistic inspiration. Water is linked with a strong colour-sense, discriminating taste, and an ability to create 'atmosphere'. While fire and air can both think of clever ideas, water is able to sustain them continuing life.

In career matters, water suggests the ability to look beneath the surface of things. An intuitive sense of direction, which is often hard to articulate, is typical of this suit. Funny feelings, and employing someone on trust are also indicated. Above all, when the suit of

Cups relates to this area of life it suggests a love of one's work, and an ability to develop talent.

A love of nature and animals is also linked to both suit and element. Pets are often important to water types, and the home is seen as a place of refuge.

This idea of home transcends bricks and mortar, for it also represents a spiritual inner home. Material comforts are often outward manifestations of the inner longing to be 'at home' with yourself, to be comfortable inside your own skin.

The suit of Cups emphasizes the importance of people and how to deal with them. Kindness and generosity towards oneself and others are key themes. Typical watery types will often attract waifs and strays, for they are soft-hearted and sensitive to others misfortunes. This tendency may sometimes create difficulties in their own lives by draining their energy.

The court cards and the element of water

The court cards of the suit of Cups are linked to the water signs of Cancer, Scorpio and Pisces. Characteristics typical of this group often manifest as obvious traits in the people represented by Cups. Sometimes adjacent cards will provide the information you need to pinpoint the exact form of behaviour or personality type. When this seems obscure or irrelevant, the cards may be representing situations. However, if you are certain they are people – which they usually are – you

can assume that the suit of Cups generally stands for emotional individuals who are often artistic, sensitive, and may be self–indulgent.

When negative, Cups represent demanding, self-pitying individuals who are simply flooded with emotion. They can also be devious, manipulative and untrustworthy.

Cancer the Crab is home-loving, sensitive, loving and moody. Cancerian moods ebb and flow with the phases of the Moon, the Sign's ruling planet. Typically, Cancerians' hard outer shell conceals a soft emotional interior, filled with memories and intuitions. Their famous tenacity can be both a blessing and a curse. On the one hand, they do not give up easily in life – and can be very successful as a result. On the other, they find it hard to let go of outworn ideas, ways of life and relationships.

When the court cards symbolize Cancerian traits, they may be representing people who are already tied to you by deep emotional bonds. Should a spread seem to concentrate on family matters, or relationships for example, then the court cards may appear as parents, spouse, or brothers and sisters. This will be true, even if these people have no water signs in their horoscopes.

Negative forms of behaviour linked to Cancerian Cups include moodiness, over-sensitivity, and possessive behaviour. If there is someone – particularly a lover or parent – who seems over-protective and smothering to you, one of the Cups is likely to represent that person in a reading.

Scorpio is a deep, dark sign traditionally linked with life's mysteries. The penetrating minds of Scorpios enjoy searching out secrets and constructing schemes. They are fiercely loyal to those they love, often psychic, and notably charismatic. When their powerful energies are flowing freely they are some of the most dynamic people you're ever likely to meet.

When the court cards represent Scorpios, or Scorpio types, they frequently highlight the magnetic qualities inherent in the sign. Thus, people who have a powerful effect upon you, or to whom you are intensely attracted may appear as Cups. The tone of the reading, and in particular the surrounding cards, should make this clear.

Negative forms of behaviour linked to Scorpio include manipulative power games, jealousy, and impenetrable secretiveness. If these are indicated elsewhere in the cards, members of the suit of Cups tend to stand for the people involved.

Pisces, symbolized by two fishes, is said to contain elements of all the other signs of the zodiac. This elusive, mystical sign is perhaps the most watery of all, for it is possessed of an extraordinarily heightened sensitivity. Poetic dreamers, Piscean Cups find it difficult to balance their beautiful visions with hard-edged reality. Kindness, self-sacrifice and artistic ability are all common traits of this sign.

The Queen of Cups often represents women who display ultra-feminine, receptive characteristics. The Knight of Cups, too, can bring a spiritual vision of love when he enters a reading. When the King of Cups is linked to Pisces, he is either very powerful or very lost. These figures tend to appear when an affair – or even idealistic business partnership – is at a very romantic, slightly unreal stage. They can also represent those who care deeply for you, or who are very much in love.

Negative forms of behaviour linked to Pisces, and Cups, include destructive emotions, unrealistic expectations, and masochism. The Cups can represent 'lost souls', who are too vulnerable to cope or are filled with self-pity. These types may resort to drink or drugs as a means of escape, or tend to cocoon themselves in a fantasy world rather than face reality.

The Ace of Wands

THE ACES

Keywords: New beginnings, power and energy

Each Ace signifies the beginning of an impulse, chain of events, or expression of a type of energy. They are dynamic cards, heralding initiative or initiation when in a positive, upright position.

In numerology, one is a masculine number which relates to the conscious mind. It symbolizes independence, confidence, and the ability to initiate schemes and get things done. This number corresponds to the Magician in the Major Arcana. The Aces represent different aspects of his go-ahead qualities.

THE ACE OF WANDS

Keywords: Optimism and invention

The Ace of Wands most commonly relates to career opportunities, and exciting new directions in working life. These may come from within in the shape of brilliant, intuitive idea, or from outside in the form of a challenging new project or job.

This Ace is expansive, optimistic and suggests that you will have all the energy you need to fulfil your ambitions. Whatever kind of work you do is about to be revitalized, and you should soon have a chance to develop your own ideas. Fruitful innovation is signalled.

Fire is a creative element. So the confident, fast-moving energy symbolized by the Ace of Wands may manifest outside your working life. You may discover a fascinating new interest, or creative hobby. You may suddenly realize that you want to paint, write, or travel, climb, play a musical instrument or study.

Fiery creativity may also express itself physically. Fertility is indicated, as is the urge to re-create yourself in the form of a child. If other cards, such as the Empress, suggest this then pregnancy and birth are likely. However, do not forget that this may also be a symbolic conception, gestation and birth.

Reversed

Keywords: Creative blocks and delays

Certainly the urge to change your circumstances is present. However, when the Ace of Wands appears in the reversed position delays are indicated. You may feel impatient and frustrated, but are unable to do anything about it.

Perhaps your creativity and intuition are blocked. Again, the surrounding cards should indicate the causes of this problem. You may have just begun a new job or project which has failed to live up to your hopes and dreams.

The Ace of Wands reversed can appear when you have been trying hard to bring something off, launch a new idea or method, or find out your true career path. At this point it seems as if all your efforts have been in vain. If this applies to you, or the subject of the reading, look carefully at the rest of the spread. It should provide some useful clues, possible directions, or suggest how or when you can change your approach.

In relationship terms the Ace of Wands reversed indicates similar blocks. These may be primarily emotional or sexual, for the Ace of Wands reversed traditionally suggests barrenness. You may feel cut off from your heart, unable to express affection – or experience this emotional desert at another's hands. Impotence and frigidity could mar your sexual relationship; there may be some trouble if trying to conceive a child.

THE ACE OF PENTACLES

Keywords: Prosperity and increase

The earthy Ace of Pentacles symbolizes concrete reality, material wealth and comforts. Some Tarot decks call this card the Ace of Coins, and this is perhaps its most evocative name for divination purposes.

When you draw this Ace in a reading, you can expect some noticeable financial improvement in your life. Money is on the way, and you will soon be more comfortable. The Aces denote new beginnings, so this change is likely to involve a new and better-paid job as well. If this seems totally unlikely, then you could receive a substantial bonus or benefit from a profit-sharing scheme.

This card also suggests windfalls, and gains through gambling. It can signify cash gifts, or other valuable presents – especially ones which relate to the home, or appeal to the senses in some way. Money received in this way is unlikely to be used for anything as mundane as paying your household bills, and may be spent with great rapidity.

While tangible cash is frequently suggested by the Ace of Pentacles, it is important to consider other meanings too. Prosperity is suggested on other levels; you may be entering a particularly productive phase. If you enjoy working with your hands, for example, you will gain great pleasure from this activity now. The things you produce may even herald the beginning of a new career, or 'cottage industry': many successful businesses were started at home.

Emotionally, the Ace of Pentacles suggests security and contentment. Relationships or working partnerships are peaceful; there is an air of solidity and permanence.

Reversed

Keywords: Material problems

Your new-found wealth may not last. Investments may prove unsound, money is lost rather than gained. If you have recently benefited financially through a new job, you may find you are not up to it, or that it is making you unhappy.

The Ace of Pentacles reversed can also mean sheer, money-grabbing

The Ace of Pentacles

greed. It suggests someone who is already financially secure, even wealthy, but who cannot resist trying to make more money – or acquire more possessions. This impulse may be based on the desire for worldly power, or perhaps stems from a poverty-stricken background. If backed up by other cards, this position may point to corrupt business dealings, embezzlement, or fraud.

The Ace of Swords

THE ACE OF SWORDS

Keywords: Powerful forces

The Ace of Swords represents the clarity and power of air. Above all, this ace signifies mental changes, fresh ways of thinking, and intellectual prowess. It can herald success – particularly in some field where unemotional, logical thought is important.

It also stands for the forces of justice, and if this meaning is appropriate to your question – or is indicated by other cards – it denotes legal matters, court cases, tax matters and so on.

Powerful influences are at work when the Ace of Swords appears. Sometimes excessive power is indicated, like an unstoppable hurricane sweeping through your life. Such energy may destroy anything which is not firmly rooted; when the wind drops much that was familiar seems to have been blown away.

This tendency for the Ace of Swords to represent excess was one of the reasons it had such a dubious traditional reputation. It also meant death, but being an airy card this refers to mental, emotional or spiritual death. Ideas or

attachments may 'die' when the Ace of Swords appears – such deaths open the gates of change and progress. As usual, look to adjacent or surrounding cards to see which area of life is especially affected.

Some sources link the Ace of Swords with the laws of karma, which are basically perceived as the laws of cause and effect. As you have sown, so you shall reap, says the law of karma; if you have sown discord and strife then it will be returned to you. Traditionally, negative forces return to their creator tripled in size and force. Those who have led blameless lives have nothing to fear!

Reversed
Keyword: Tension

When the Ace of Swords appears reversed you can expect delays, misunderstandings, or even documents mislaid in the post. An invisible puppet master seems to be pulling the strings, delighting in destroying your expectations, plans, or schemes. All of this will probably seem very unfair.

Quarrels are also indicated. However, if you consider that these are one – often positive – way to clear the air, you may be able to take a sanguine view of them. Old, negative links may be sever and, typically, cutting words are the most likely means to achieve this.

Physically, the Ace of Swords reversed suggests mental stress and imbalance. You could find yourself up against someone powerful and tyrannical, or be inclined to behave this way yourself.

THE ACE OF CUPS

Keywords: Love and creativity

The Ace of Cups is overflowing with the waters of love and creativity. It signifies joy, happiness, love and deep, abiding friendships. It also represents the well-springs of creativity and self-expression. Fire and water are both creative elements, but while fire seizes bright ideas from nowhere, water conceives and nurtures them.

When you draw the Ace of Cups in a spread, you are about to be inspired. Such inspiration may come through a new, important love affair, or be sparked off through colourful, vivid dreams.

If you, or the subject of the reading, are concerned about career matters this card indicates an extremely productive phase. Fulfilling projects, meaningful achievements and, very possibly, good emotional rapport with colleagues are all suggested here.

Emotionally, the Ace of Cups is literally in its element. Your heart opens to another, special person. Mutual passion is experienced, and uplifting joyful emotions characterize your relationship. If you are already seriously involved, this card suggests an exceptionally loving phase. Babies may be conceived or born, gifts received, friendships strengthened.

Reversed

Keywords: Emotional upheaval

The Cup is empty, its contents overturned and spilt. You, or someone close, may be running away from your feelings. A love affair could be coming to an end, with attendant emotional upheaval.

This position can sometimes signify an unrealistic love affair, which has been rather one-sided. One person has poured out love and affection, the other has taken without contributing very much. One partner may be out of touch with his or her emotions, and so the relationship is unable to deepen and flourish.

In terms of self-expression, this card denotes blocked creativity. This is also true of the Ace of Wands reversed. But in this case the block is more likely to stem from emotional stress, or a feeling of being 'used up' and dry in some way.

Sterility, physical, mental or emotional is traditionally denoted by this position. There is a deep need for some tender, loving care.

The Ace of Cups

THE TWOS

Keywords: Balance and synthesis

The number two represents balance and harmony. It may be visualized as masculine and feminine; light and dark; yin and yang; and all polar opposites. In numerology, two is a feminine number which symbolizes the urge to nurture, receive, and synthesize opposites – blending them into a perfect whole. The twos correspond to the High Priestess in the Major Arcana, and echo her receptive qualities. Their basic, underlying theme is one of union.

THE TWO OF WANDS

Keywords: Balanced enterprise and power

A successful and prosperous partnership is often suggested by the two of Wands. The fiery qualities of this card indicate a productive meeting of minds, and may also signify a rewarding friendship formed through work.

The two of Wands can also represent a powerful businessman or woman. This person usually controls a company, or other team of people, and has achieved great career success, is influential, and often well-respected in his or her field.

When the two of Wands suggests an

event it is often connected with property matters. All negotiations connected to buying and selling property are under favourable influences; you are able to sign contracts without a hitch. Deals will work out in your favour – you may make more money than you are expecting.

Reversed

Keywords: Partnership problems

Business, creative or even financial partnerships may be causing problems. The people involved are unable to enjoy their success – they may want more; or else it seems hollow and meaningless.

This position suggests that partnerships relating to career and money may be coming to an end.

If involved with property transactions, be prepared for delays, unforeseen expenses, and other disappointments. Some of these may be totally unexpected; the lawyer contacts you on the very day you are supposed to be concluding a deal and changes the arrangements.

There could be a stubborn, proud individual holding matters up, or causing you problems. Such a person is likely to be well-educated or of professional standing. But for all his or her intelligence, an inability to adapt, or see other people's viewpoint prevails.

THE TWO OF PENTACLES

Keywords: Financial balance and fluctuating fortunes

Some kind of financial, material or practical balancing act is signified by the two of Pentacles. You may have to take

The Two of Wands

The Two of Pentacles

on extra work in order to pay for a holiday, or special treat. You find yourself juggling two bank accounts or earning two sources of income.

It is quite likely that some money will be made available shortly, or you will soon receive practical help which will enable you to pursue a particular project.

Because this is a dual card, there is a double meaning and a warning. When this help materializes, do not abuse or ignore it. You are being given a chance to develop a second string to your bow.

The two of Pentacles often refers to self-employed people who have uncertain incomes. There may be too much work, or not enough, and these people must learn to balance their energies and resources accordingly.

If other cards confirm it, this card can also signify restlessness at work or at home. Again this can be due to fluctuating fortunes – you may find that you are entertaining lavishly one month, and living on bread and spaghetti the next.

Reversed

Keyword: Duality

The two of Pentacles reversed issues a warning against living beyond your means; financial imbalance, mounting debts, and wild fluctuations are suggested here.

Psychologically, this position denotes a touchy, moody phase where you are easily upset or depressed. Here duality indicates that these black moments will be 'balanced' by periods of feeling overconfident.

If your spread concerns work or career, the two of Pentacles reversed denotes unstable or inconsistent action. There does not seem to be anything fundamentally wrong, but you – or the subject of the reading – are somewhat aimless and therefore going nowhere at the moment. Fixity of purpose is required if the matter at hand is to be completed satisfactorily.

THE TWO OF SWORDS

Keywords: Justice and tension

The two of Swords represents balanced forces. But these forces are balanced in such a way that there is a sense of stalemate, and the underlying message of the card suggests tension.

When you see this card in a spread it can signify peace after a troubled period. Yet it is an uneasy peace, there is something unsettled about it, and the original tensions which gave rise to the problem are still lingering. These will have to be resolved. So, the two of Swords may herald the calm before, during or after the storm. The storm itself should be suggested by other cards.

If you consulted the cards about an essentially practical matter, such as a law suit, or negotiations of some kind, then the two of Swords promises resolution. Justice will be done. In this respect, the two of Swords is a lesser manifestation of the card Justice in the Major Arcana. If such a problem has been causing you sleepless nights, you will soon be able to stop worrying — relief is in sight.

Psychologically, the card suggests someone who wants peace at any price. This is often characteristic of the astrological sign Libra, which corresponds to the two of Swords. You, or someone in your life, is unwilling to confront existing problems — fearing rows, separations, or other 'imbalances'. Messy and uncontrollable emotions may lurk just beneath the surface of the situation, but they are being ignored and repressed.

The Two of Swords

Reversed
Keywords: Take care

The two of Swords reversed is telling you to think very carefully. While it can denote release and resolution, such positive changes require careful handling now. You may not be receiving the best advice, so do not rush into anything impulsively — or sign documents without reading the smallest of small print.

This position also denotes lies and deceit. Someone may be trying to take advantage of you, and encouraging you to change direction for his or her own benefit. Or, of course, you may be guilty of doing this yourself. There is certainly a very self-centred aspect to this card, other people's feelings have not been considered.

The most positive meaning of the two of Swords reversed is slow change, and release from captivity of any kind. As always, surrounding cards should suggest to which area of life this influence applies.

THE TWO OF CUPS
Keywords: Partnership and commitment

The two of Cups represents love, harmony and partnership. It signifies the blending of male and female. This beautiful and positive card primarily denotes love and affection in a relationship. Frequently it suggests a new romantic attachment entering your life, or a delightfully loving phase if you are already in an established partnership.

When symbolizing an important love

affair, however, it is more than likely to be backed up by other cards which will amplify the message. And, of course, when it appears in answer to some question about love it is telling you that there will be someone special soon. It is important to look carefully at your spread when this card appears, for it can also mean happy partnerships of a different kind.

If surrounded by 'work' or 'career' cards the two of Cups represents an harmonious and creative working partnership. A deep friendship could well develop between the two partners; mental and emotional sympathy is indicated, and a very productive union should result.

If neither of these two meanings seems appropriate, consider social life. This card may be pointing to a particularly joyful patch. Friendships flourish, you meet congenial people, there is warmth and laughter.

Below: The Two of Cups

Reversed
Keywords: Emotional imbalance

Emotional battles are suggested when the two of Cups is reversed. Relationships are turned upside down, beset with difficulties, and filled with arguments. Neither side seems able to understand the other.

Similarly, this position can denote an imbalance within the relationship. One person may love more than the other, or at least be able to express love more freely.

A separation is likely; other cards should indicate whether this is likely to be permanent or temporary. A working partnership or marriage could be dissolved at this time. However, since the two of Cups suggests foolish waste, separation might not prove the correct course of action in the long term.

It would also be foolish to assume automatically that this position means divorce or separation without checking to see what other cards say. If you are at all uncertain, emotional disharmony is the most you should read into this card.

THE THREES

Keywords: Creative growth

Three is the number of growth and success. It is a creative, active number which combines the impetus of one, the receptivity and balancing qualities of two, and their successful, productive fusion.

This magical number was often regarded as sacred, and there are many examples of religious trinities –including the triple-faced goddess herself as virgin, mother and crone. Other mythical links include triple-headed Cerberus, the fearsome hound who guarded the gates of Hades; the three Graces; the numerous tridents which crop up in world mythology. This number corresponds to the Empress in the Major Arcana, and these cards carry a similarly fertile vibration.

stead. You will be able to build something up now, or develop your skills and ideas further.

Sometimes this card signifies a helpful, often successful individual who is about to enter your life. This person will offer you advice and practical assistance, very often in the form of a job offer or other opportunity.

An established business could bear fruit at this time. This may be in the form of increased profits, new directions and initiatives, beneficial partnerships or mergers.

On any level concerned with creativity or communication, dreams can be turned into reality. The three of Wands is a very positive card for writers, speakers, inventors, and those involved in commerce.

THE THREE OF WANDS

Keywords: Opportunities and success

The three of Wands fortells success – especially in business ventures, or creative endeavours. Whatever was begun by the Ace, and nurtured by the two, is now ready to expand and bear fruit. The ground has already been prepared when this card appears, and the overall feeling is, 'what's next?'.

If your spread specifically concerned career, this card denotes new opportunities coming your way. Such opportunities are generally linked to whatever you have been involved with previously. Past experience, contacts, friendships and initiative will stand you in good

Reversed

Keywords: Lost opportunity

Opportunities may be lost due to obstinacy and arrogance. Foolish pride could be a serious obstacle to success when the three of Wands appears reversed. Job offers, or other career possibilities can be jeopardized by a stubborn kind of independence. There may even be overtones of snobbery here – the 'this is beneath me' kind of attitude.

When this card indicates the failure of a project, it is generally for two reasons. Either the venture was over-ambitious, or those involved failed to get their ideas across in practical terms. Dreams are still-born here, and cannot find their way into material reality at this point.

Left: The Three of Wands

THE THREE OF PENTACLES

Keywords: Success through skill

The three of Pentacles is associated – like Wands – with work, but has a more practical interpretation. Here, someone has worked hard to master a profession, art, or other means of earning a living. The time and effort put in has increased the person's value in the market-place, for he or she is now confident and on the way to becoming established.

This card suggests that all this effort will be rewarded shortly. The reward may take the form of promotion, a salary increase or, at the very least, praise and approval from others. However, since this is an earthy card, material gain of some kind is the most likely – although do not expect large sums.

If your questions concerned the home, this card denotes improvements and decorations. You may be getting the builders in to create an extension to your home; about to have a new kitchen fitted; or even to have the garden landscaped. The money to pay for this is available, and increased comfort is generally signified.

Left: The Three of Pentacles
Right: The Three of Swords

Reversed

Keywords: Blocked success

The three of Pentacles reversed tells of potential success spoilt by lack of application or enterprise. Fear or failure, or being exceptionally fixed in one's ways are the most likely blocks to be overcome here.

This position suggests a sadly 'stick in the mud' attitude, highly appropriate for an earthy card. Originality is stifled, talent disregarded, and security prized above all.

If you were hoping for a salary increase, you are unlikely to receive one just now. This is unlikely to have much to do with your abilities, but reflects a penny-pinching attitude on the part of your employers or clients.

THE THREE OF SWORDS

Keyword: Heartache

The three of Swords usually brings tears in its wake. Yet these are often preceded by romantic interludes and irresistible sexual attractions. Such alliances may seem very real at first, but rarely develop into anything deeper.

Sometimes this card suggests 'the eternal triangle', in which at least one of the participants must inevitably get hurt in the end. Relationships foretold by this card are often very much in the mind. Those involved are, in fact, seeking something beyond themselves –

and think they have found it for a time in another person.

This does not in any way decrease the association's power, for while it is going on it is likely to be obsessive. However, enlightenment may come out of this painful episode, or it could act as a catalyst in your life. Remember the overall creativity of the threes. Yes, this is a difficult card – but it still heralds growth as an end result.

If you are already involved, this card suggests your current relationship is on rocky ground and may be coming to an end – certainly in its present form. It is probably causing you great mental stress, and there is likely to be considerable conflict between you. Separation is likely; other cards will indicate whether this is final.

Occasionally, this card signifies inevitable separations – such as those caused by career. One partner may have to spend some time away on a job, or studying. This can be a challenge for both people.

Physically, there may be a great tension present when this card appears, for it denotes inner conflict.

When applying to career matters, the three of Swords means disruption. People working in groups may experience a troubled time when no-one seems to be able to get on with anyone else. However, if these storms can be weathered new and constructive ideas may result.

Reversed

Keyword: Disorder

Confusion and anxiety are denoted by the three of Swords reversed. Things are disordered, chaos and upheaval may be stress-factors in your life. These meanings may be applied to practical matters, emotions, or mental processes – adjacent cards should make this clear. However, it should be remembered that every dark and chaotic situation contains the potential for rebirth.

This reversed position also indicates that the major heartache, signified by its upright face, is over. Although there is still a lot to be dealt with before total equilibrium is restored, the healing process has begun when this card appears reversed – even if it doesn't seem like it.

THE THREE OF CUPS

Keywords: Celebration and renewal

The three of Cups is a light–hearted, joyful and expansive card. You can certainly smile when you receive it, for there is likely to be something to celebrate soon.

This card, not surprisingly, often relates to personal life. It denotes family celebrations, such as engagements, weddings, christenings, and special anniversaries. It can sometimes herald a birth – although when it does, it is usually for a close friend or relation outside the immediate family circle.

It is a lucky card, denoting vital forces, glowing good health, and the possibility of presents and prizes. There is happiness ahead; joy seems to act like a magnet, and draw more good things to it at this time.

Socially, the three of Cups signifies a lively phase with plenty of parties and

The Three
of Cups

happy events. You will enjoy dressing up for these occasions, and there is much fun and laughter all around you. Make the most of it!

Reversed

Keywords: Over the top

Over-indulgence or too much socializing are likely when the three of Cups is reversed. You could find yourself putting on weight, or feeling rather unhealthy as a result.

Financially, this card warns you not to be over-extravagant. You are likely to want to spend money like water – especially on fun and entertainment. The urge to indulge yourself buying presents on credit can be compulsive and there is an analogy here between financial and emotional over-expenditure. This card may well appear in many spreads after Christmas, classic season of overdoing it in many countries.

At its most benevolent, the three of Cups reversed echoes its upright position. There is little likelihood of a birth or wedding, but there may still be plenty of parties and a generally good – if less sparkling – atmosphere prevails.

THE FOURS

Keywords: Stability and restriction

Four is an earthy, stable number. It corresponds to the positive qualities of structure, logic, authority, and endurance. It has been pointed out that many of the ancient names meaning 'deity' had four letters: Latin Deus; Egyptian Amun; Sumerian Jabe; and Assyrian Adad being a few examples.

Linked with the Emperor of the Major Arcana, the fours represent the idea of foundation and form. Yet this structure can also signify restriction, or the realization that our dreams are too wild to come true. Very often this is a positive realization, prompting a more down-to-earth approach to our lives.

Indeed, without structure visions and ideas would never materialize. Every piece of music requires an instrument; artists must grapple with paint and canvas; inventors must demonstrate how their ideas might work in reality. However, many people find structure, and the self-discipline which accompanies it, very hard to handle. So, depending upon personality, the fours may be seen as strong and constructive – or dull and limiting. They are, in fact, capable of being both.

THE FOUR OF WANDS

Keywords: Harvest and prosperity

In the four of Wands, the stability of four expresses itself in a fiery way. Since fire is an expansive element, this card represents a successful and abundant harvest, and also signifies a well-earned rest. Some project or period of hard work has preceded this moment, you can now sit back for a little while and enjoy the fruits of your labours. This harvest is often translated into material terms; the four of Wands suggests moving into a new home, or even acquiring a second home – which has been worked for and dreamt of for a long time. Here, the idea of home has an uplifting, celebratory quality. Such a place will be much loved, and lots of energy and imagination will go into any renovations which need to be done.

A powerful sense of security is signified by this card. This may manifest as an intuitive feeling of faith in yourself, a sense of inner harmony. It bodes well for current and future projects; there is a firm foundation upon which to build. Mentally, the four of Wands indicates that reasoning abilities are productively combined with intuition.

In terms of career, the four of Wands relates to work in property, theatre, entertainment, music, and dance.

The Four
of Wands

A reversed four of Wands can also signify a rest or break of some kind, particularly in your career. At the time, this may be worrying, and you could be anxious to learn where the next job is coming from. Soon you will look back on this period with a certain amount of longing, for a busy phase lies just ahead.

Reversed

Keywords: Delayed success

Any kind of completion or conclusion is likely to be delayed. It will still take place, but you may have to be patient for a little longer. This is especially true of property matters, but do not lose heart for this card does not suggest failure.

You may be trying to run faster than you can walk. The four of Wands reversed sometimes denotes anxiety and nervous energy which is unnecessary, and may be causing difficulties. The old saying 'Rome was not built in a day' is appropriate here.

FOUR OF PENTACLES
Keywords: Financial security

The four of Pentacles denotes, above all, that there will soon be money in the bank. A period of financial stability is coming, and you should be able to make some lasting improvements to your circumstances – perhaps through sensible investments. The four of Pentacles does not indicate fabulous wealth, but speaks of continuing comfort and an income which covers all your outgoings and leaves you with sufficient cash to enjoy yourself too.

When it relates to work, it usually suggests a slow-but-sure increase in power and responsibility. Improvements and advancements are lasting, but made in a gradual way. There is nothing exciting, sudden or lucky about them.

Socially, this card can sometimes indicate a 'social climber', snob, or someone who judges people by what they own, rather than what they are. Such a person may prefer to befriend wealthy people, believing that they are in some way 'better' than others.

Reversed

Keywords: Money, money, money

Money, and thoughts of money are dominating matters. The four of Pentacles reversed is a rather unpleasant card, suggesting greed and a miserly spirit. At its most positive, it denotes financial anxiety. Perhaps the querent feels burdened by monetary responsibilities, and is constantly trying to balance the household budget.

When this card refers to an aspect of personality, it signifies avarice, envy, and discontent. Nothing is good enough, nothing is perfect, and nothing is enjoyed simply for itself. This person is

Above: The Four of Pentacles

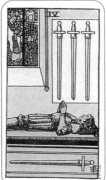

Below: The Four of Swords

so busy hanging on to what he or she has got, there is a danger of being dominated by material possessions – or trapped by financial success.

THE FOUR OF SWORDS

Keywords: Rest and recuperation

The four of Swords expresses the idea of stability through rest. As you can imagine, stability is a quality not naturally found in this mental, airy element. So here, the somewhat solid vibrations of four should be interpreted in a temporary way. Rest and recuperation are required when you draw this card in a reading. A quiet time allows you to gather your thoughts, re-assess what has been already achieved, and enjoy a peaceful interlude.

Sometimes this card indicates actual physical convalescence after an illness. But very often, this illness may be traced back to a time of extreme mental pressure; it is a fairly desperate plea for peace and quiet.

It can also foretell a short stay in hospital; a planned retreat to a health farm or religious sanctuary; or a deliberate withdrawal from the world, for a time. The four of Swords should always be taken seriously; unplug the telephone, stop going out every   night, and take it easy for a while. This card may be accompanied by the Hermit, which serves to strengthen its message.

Reversed

Keywords: Enforced rest

Earlier warnings have been ignored.

Instead of choosing to withdraw, withdrawal is being forced upon you.

In health terms, a more serious stay in hospital is suggested here. Nervous exhaustion over a prolonged period has caused some physical problem, or mental instability.

Socially and personally you may find yourself rather lonely. Friendships and relationships fail to bring pleasure; people who were once close to you seem to have changed. Your private life could seem dull and limited; it is only a phase however, and will not last forever.

THE FOUR OF CUPS

Keywords: Emotional re-evaluation

The four of Cups stresses the limitations of its ruling number. Here, someone has allowed stagnation and boredom to get in – especially on the emotional level. Feelings no longer flow, and a vague sense of dissatisfaction prevails – either with oneself, or with relationships, friendships, and colleagues.

There could be a mild depression when this card appears. Perhaps things have been too secure for too long. New interests, friendships and activities are required, but the querent feels too tired and self-absorbed to look for them. A short holiday would be beneficial at this time; even a long week-end away from normal surroundings may prove helpful.

Sometimes this card appears when the querent has been emotionally scarred, and is frightened of risking getting hurt again. Love is being offered, there is the chance of a relationship developing – but doubt and uncertainty

Right: The Four of Cups

are preventing the link from flourishing. A misguided need for security, based on fear, is preventing risks being taken.

In established relationships, it may be time to re-evaluate spend time together doing enjoyable things, and put some fresh energy into something which has grown rather soggy.

Reversed

Keywords: Fear of being alone

A horrible and pervasive fear of being alone creates the impetus for a frantic social life, or string of unsuitable lovers. There is small pleasure to be had from this frenetic pleasure-seeking; it is ultimately unsatisfactory.

When career matters are at stake, this card suggests that your current projects – or even profession – mean little to you. Perhaps you used to enjoy them, but have now outgrown them and are seeking a challenge. You may have needed the security and sense of continuity the work once provided. Now is the time to look for new opportunities, or consider training for a new career. Other cards should reveal whether this is a passing phase, or heralds an important turning point in your life. You might need something as simple as a new hobby or interest – especially if creative abilities are underused at work.

THE FIVES

Keywords: Change through strife

Five represents the need to be free of the restrictions symbolized by four. This number is linked with the magical pentagram, which has five points. These represent the four elements plus the invisible fifth: ether, spirit, pure energy.

This magical pentagram may be used in ritual to banish or invoke, depending upon the way it is drawn. Similarly, the fives in Tarot may bring welcome changes which one struggles to institute, or seem to represent destructive forces which drive away valued relationships or situations.

Superstitious people regard this number as either very lucky or as the number favoured by demons. Ancient Romans were said to incorporate this number in a talisman designed to repel evil forces. It is an extraordinarily complex number, often regarded as unfortunate and destructive.

Certainly, each of the fives in the Minor Arcana represents difficult situations, pain and struggles of various kinds. Yet these battles must be fought, sorrow and hard times must be endured. But once these things have been overcome positive changes can be welcomed.

Five corresponds with the Hierophant, or Pope, in the Major Arcana. This card represents convention, and when reversed embodies the forces of anarchy. The need to break out, to progress and overturn existing situations is a common theme which links all the fives to the reversed face of the Hierophant.

Right: The Five of Wands
Far right: The Five of Pentacles

THE FIVE OF WANDS

Keywords: War games

In the Waite deck, the five of Wands depicts a kind of mock battle. This is being fought with staves, but nobody seems to be getting badly hurt; it resembles a game.

When you draw the five of Wands, the energetic qualities of fire are expressed in a competitive way. This is a testing time, and does involve a battle, yet the conflict retains elements of a game for it is fiery. While things may become almost too hot to handle, they are challenging and the urge to win will be very strong on both sides.

In any area of your life you may expect opposition, or power struggles of some kind. You may experience this within yourself, discovering new and uncomfortable desires and ambitions in the process. Views differ, arguments arise, and sparks fly. There is plenty of adrenalin around, and likely to be plenty of rows as well. However, none of this should be seen as damaging in retrospect; a finer product or set of ideas is being forged.

Reversed

Keyword: Disputes

Litigation is a common meaning when the five of Wands is reversed. Disputes and wrangles are likely to be resolved in court, or through legal negotiations. Always check to see if this is backed up by other cards, however.

Psychologically, this card can represent inner conflict and an inability to reach a decision. Such conflict is likely to contain some anger; this is not being expressed directly and may emerge in dreams, or sudden outbursts of temper.

If surrounded by positive cards, the five of Wands reversed heralds victory. Your struggles are nearly over, although everything may still feel very fragile for a time.

THE FIVE OF PENTACLES

Keywords: Loss of faith, poverty

This is a very difficult card to read for someone, for nine times out of ten it indicates a period of financial loss, or hardship. This depressing time may have been caused by past extravagance – especially in business matters. Alternatively, a period of unemployment has eaten into material resources and there is little money to play with.

These losses, or experience of poverty are likely to be accompanied by a loss of faith in oneself. Hardship and struggle have worn down optimism, the daily grind and battle for survival seem to take every ounce of energy available.

Should the five of Pentacles appear when financial hardship seems out of the question, it indicates a poverty of spirit. Low self-worth is the enemy here; confidence and creativity are seriously depleted.

When this card appears it is essential to look carefully at the rest of the spread, for a solution to this problem is at hand. It is unlikely to be an easy solution, because conflict is inherent in all the fives. But it should be possible to rebuilt a career, home, and sense of financial security from the ruins denoted by the five of Pentacles.

Restoration of faith and confidence is, of course, the most important thing of all. An optimistic and helpful Tarot reading may help to put someone on the right track. Because the fives represent change, this situation may eventually result in something of lasting value. The struggles will have been worth it.

Reversed

Keyword: Restoration

You will have to work hard, but your financial situation should soon improve. Former losses will be made good, and you could receive help from an outside source – possibly a grant to enable you to set up a new business.

Faith and confidence are growing, although the memory of this difficult time in your life may fade very gradually.

THE FIVE OF SWORDS

Keywords: Limitation and power

The five of Swords again highlights the theme of battle, enemies and change which runs through the fives. It is a complex card, and its meaning must be carefully considered as part of the pattern of a reading.

It can often indicate failure and loss of some kind. In this context the querent may be experiencing a loss, or has been the cause of loss or failure in another's life. This should be clear from surrounding cards, or from the five of swords' own position in a spread.

When these endings refer to the querent, they are usually accompanied by a sense of being limited in some way. However, from these limitations and apparent unfairness a new direction will come. The querent will be able to pick up the shattered pieces, and create something new – and perhaps more realistic.

Sometimes, the five of Swords denotes underhand tactics. Lies, gossip, and malice could be the cause of defeat, or have been employed by the querent to gain some kind of hollow victory.

When surrounded by positive cards, the five of Swords indicates that any loss or disappointment sustained is minor. The path you were following was not for you, and the only thing that has been wounded is your pride.

Reversed

Keywords: A battle of wills

The five of swords reversed signifies defeat after a battle of wills. Because it is an airy card, this battle is likely to have been fought with words – including lies and slander.

It may be very hard for you to accept this defeat, to let go of the negative feel-ings it has created. There may be powerful feelings of jealousy, envy, and self-pity to overcome. But the battle is over, it has been fought and won, and there is no going back. Analysing what went wrong, or blaming others will not put back the clock. It is better to accept this episode, and resolve to start afresh.

THE FIVE OF CUPS

Keywords: Something lost and something gained

The five of Cups is a sad card which denotes grieving and emotional wounds. Some ideal relationship, deeply-held belief, or even faith in another has been dashed to the ground. The cup is spilled, and its fertile contents wasted.

However, there is more to this card than melancholy regrets and broken dreams. Something has indeed been lost, yet something remains – which will soon be discovered. This suggests that you, or the querent, may be harking back to old wounds and are, at present, unable to release them. There is a sense of despair, and an inability to understand why or when things went wrong. At the same time, this card is telling you that in your heart of hearts you know there are other avenues to explore.

When this card refers to an ongoing relationship, it suggests that some vow has been broken or that there has been some kind of betrayal. This does not necessarily mean an affair outside the relationship. It can indicate disappointment with one's partner on some level, or a feeling of emotional loneliness and waste within the relationship. Perhaps one partner is more demonstrative or supportive than the other – or certainly sees things this way, whether this is true of false.

Reversed
Keywords: Cautious hope

An unhappy time is coming to an end soon. The black clouds of despair are lifting, hope rises and new opportunities appear. Pain and struggle have left their mark, however, and newly-optimistic feelings may be more cautious and restrained than they were before.

Sometimes this card represents happiness coming back into your life in the form of a dear friend or former lover. You may have parted badly, and the relationship could have caused you pain and regret. Now you can make up your differences, and restore the relationship between you.

Right: The Six of Wands

Left: The Five of Cups

THE SIXES
Keywords: The beginnings of harmony

Six is the mystical number of the planet Venus, which is traditionally the planet of love, harmony, peace and beauty.

The sixes of the Minor Arcana reflect these auspicious meanings, and are generally considered favourable, positive cards.

However, Venus/Aphrodite has another, more troublesome face which is often glossed over these days. She was capricious, flirtatious, and enjoyed making trouble. Her wonderful gifts and visitations to love-hungry mortals often had a sting in their tail, or preceded a sudden reversal of fortune.

Similarly, the sixes of the Tarot herald success, contentment and harmony but hint at underlying tensions, sacrifice and effort. There are riches and blessings to be had, but they may prove temporary or illusory. The sixes are linked to the Lovers in the Major Arcana, a card of love, and harmony which is also, significantly, a card of choice, or two paths.

THE SIX OF WANDS
Keyword: Victory

After the battlefield represented by the five of Wands, the six promises victory and success. This shining moment has not been easily won, however. Much effort has gone into securing it. Being a fiery card, the six of Wands suggests successful negotiations, requiring tact, knowledge and intuition to bring them to a conclusion. The right action has been taken, and you are about to reap the rewards.

Primarily, this card relates to business and career matters and can signal a well-deserved promotion, or signifies legal triumphs and sought-after contracts.

In a general sense the six of Wands augurs good news for yourself, or another. Again, this is most likely to be in business or relate to creative work endeavours.

Reversed

Keywords: Trouble at work

The six of Wands reversed warns against difficulties caused by other people. These usually relate to work; you may have to redo someone else's work before it is acceptable, or find that the person has let you down and failed to deliver what was promised.

If you are seeking promotion, do not expect to succeed at this point. Someone else is likely to get the job. In general, this card denotes trouble and argument at work, you are not going to get very far in the immediate future. This is not a good time to forge ahead, bide your time and do what you can until circumstances improve.

THE SIX OF PENTACLES

Keywords: Gifts given and received

The six of Pentacles represents gifts, philanthropy and charity. On a simple level, it indicates that you will soon be receiving some unearned money or other kind of valuable present. You could benefit from a trust or charity, or receive a pleasant – and often unexpected – legacy.

If you are struggling to establish yourself in your career, the six of Pentacles augurs solid, practical help of some kind. An established person or organization will be able to help you, either financially or by providing you with clients, a work-space, or valuable introductions. Progress will be facilitated in some way.

For those who are already established, this card suggests awards, cash prizes, and an increase in power and influence.

In the latter case, you may be in a position to help someone who is just starting out. Beware of using this power to manipulate or control someone less experienced.

Reversed

Keywords: Material loss

A warning against financial loss. This could be through stupidity, gambling, or extravagance. It may also come about through theft, or even absent-mindedness.

You may forget to put your purse in a safe place; leave your handbag on the floor of a restaurant; forget to lock up your house. Thieves help themselves to your money, or material goods.

If other cards suggest it, the six of Pentacles reversed also denotes financial settlements. These are usually connected with legal matters such as wills, divorce, or the end of a business arrangement. This meaning includes the sharing out of belongings, furniture, and other material possessions.

THE SIX OF SWORDS

Keywords: Movement restores harmony

The six of Swords is one of the most peaceful cards in this troubled suit. It suggests that you are leaving your worries behind, and moving forward into a happier phase.

This movement may relate to any area of life – surrounding cards should make this clear. An unhappy relationship is improving; financial difficulties are less pressing; an anxious, worrying period is drawing to a close.

Movement and journeys on the physical plane are indicated too. This card often augurs travel of some kind. Journeys denoted by the six of Swords are distinguished by the fact that they frequently mark the end of a hard time. They can also be restorative, and help you to think clearly about the future. Peace and balance should be renewed upon your return from the trip.

Sometimes, this kind of travel is offered as a suggestion; a short holiday may be just what is required after a period of prolonged stress, for example.

Reversed
Keyword: Tenacity

The six of Swords reversed augurs continuing difficulties, which should be of a temporary nature. However, there are still battles to be fought, and obstacles to be overcome before your life can be said to be running smoothly.

The good news is that this card does not speak of defeat, and so victory may still be possible. There is no need to abandon hope. But it should be stressed that tenacity and guts are required now.

In addition, the six of Swords reversed sometimes denotes a temporary truce, a peaceful interlude during a time of struggle. Financial problems may be ameliorated by re-mortgaging your home, securing a loan, or even selling up and moving somewhere less expensive. Of course, all these solutions require some kind of sacrifice, but serve to relieve pressure in the long term.

THE SIX OF CUPS
Keyword: Happy memories

The six of Cups is strongly linked to your past – especially your emotional past. It denotes happy childhood memories, past lovers, and old friends or special colleagues.

These past connections are now about to serve some useful purpose in the present. On a practical level, some

Above left: The Six of Pentacles
Above right: The Six of Swords

Above: The Six of Cups

former contact of yours will be in touch soon. There may be an offer of work, some kind of inspiring meeting or important introduction coming through such a person.

Emotionally, a past lover could be coming back into your life, or you could renew a former friendship. These former relationships may simply renew themselves, or serve as a bridge to new ones. Other cards will clarify this.

If the question was specifically work-orientated then the six of Cups can also indicate past efforts being rewarded. You, and your work, have been valued by an individual or company in the past. This association should now bear fruit.

On an inner level, this card can be telling you that the answer to your question lies in the past. Talents you had at school, or in earlier years, could be successfully applied to present endeavours. If you are uncertain about what to do, try to remember what made you happy in the past. Hobbies and interests you used to enjoy could offer valuable clues for future fulfilment.

Reversed

Keywords: Cutting the cords

Now is the time to cut the cords which bind you to the past. The past is holding you back in some way, and blocking your progress.

Frequently, this card indicates that nostalgia and sentimentality are clouding your vision. The past you see never really existed. This rosy vision is not only unrealistic, but has the effect of smothering your ability to move forward creatively and emotionally.

Sometimes it suggests that the memories in question are not so rosy. Perhaps your schooldays were difficult, or your family background was unsupportive. There is a tendency to blame all your problems on this less-than-perfect beginning, and so little is achieved.

A fresh start is required when you draw this card reversed, plus a concerted effort to live in the present.

Above: The Seven of Wands

THE SEVENS

Keywords: What goes up must come down

Seven is un unstable, mutable and feminine number. It often refers to inner journeys, thinking and meditation. Seven has magical, mystical overtones too. The seventh child of a seventh child is traditionally believed to possess psychic powers; there were seven planets in ancient astrology — before the discoveries of Uranus, Neptune and Pluto.

Seven can hint at unconscious or repressed talents, and is also a number which has often been linked with progress and change. The Seven Ages of Man, for instance, describes our progress from birth to death. Every cell in our bodies is said to renew itself completely within an ongoing seven-year cycle. And few people have not heard of the 'Seven-Year Itch'.

Seven is linked with the Chariot in the Major Arcana. Success, honours, victory and rewards for hard work are common meanings attributed to this card. Similarly, the sevens in the Minor Arcana can herald success, or point to the need for hard work.

Yet there is something temporary, illusory, or unstable about all the sevens. This message is also found in the Chariot, for it warns against excessive pride during the moment of victory. Time passes, and we cannot hang on to our triumph forever.

THE SEVEN OF WANDS

Keywords: Stand up for your rights

While the five of Wands augurs open battle, the seven is more like a siege. It denotes a struggle, but this time great tenacity is required. If such strength of character can be found, the battle will be won and all the obstacles overcome in the end.

It is important to stress the prospect of victory, for this card often appears when someone is just about to give up. 'I can't fight anymore, everything is against me, it's no use', is the overall feeling suggested here. To be told that there is yet more opposition seems cruel and negative. Yet with a little more effort, and firm faith in the future success is assured. Do not abandon your struggle when you receive this card, you are nearly there.

Reversed

Keywords: He who hesitates is lost

The seven of Wands reversed denotes insecurity, hesitation and fear. It says 'he who hesitates is lost' loudly and clearly. Here is a warning against losing some golden opportunity because you are afraid to take a risk.

It can also refer to wasted talents and creative abilities. These are about to be lost — not through laziness — but through fear of failing. It seems easier not to risk anything. There is a strong possibility that fear of success and or commitment may be a problem that needs facing.

Encouragement is required if the querent is to make a necessary decision. Failure to take this step will result in regret at a later date.

THE SEVEN OF PENTACLES

Keyword: Gestation

The seven of Pentacles denotes many

worries often accompanying a period of very hard work. A loan may have been taken out to finance a new career or business venture, and you are concerned about how to pay it back. There is plenty of work, but it is not paying very well.

However, many of these fears are groundless in the long term. If you are doing work which brings fulfilment, it will expand and grow. This card points to slow growth; the seeds have been sown but there is no sign as yet that they have germinated.

In the immediate present, the seven of Pentacles points to a tiring time, when you work and work for little monetary gain. It may seem pointless. Sometimes it seems as if you have thrown your money or talents away. Yet these disappointments are usually illusory, and your worries or fears are groundless.

When other cards suggest it, this card relates to unpaid 'work' such as absorbing hobbies, the work of bringing up children, or charity work. Here again, such effort may sometimes seem exhausting or depressing. But it is fundamentally satisfying and productive on non-material levels.

Reversed

Keyword: Reassessment

The seven of Pentacles reversed denotes similar worries about money and career. Hard work for little reward is also suggested, but there is an increased sense of disappointment and failure. Nothing tangible is being produced; all your hard work seems to have been in vain.

This dreary period should be ended shortly. Your attitudes towards money may undergo a positive change, and an increased sense of self-worth and practicality will help you assert yourself in this area. Do not exhaust yourself any further, either by worrying about money or by slaving away fruitlessly. Reassess your talents, dreams and direction, and prepare to start again.

THE SEVEN OF SWORDS

Keywords: Variable effort and caution

The seven of Swords is a curious, restless card. When positive, it suggests new ideas, fresh mental input at work, and general movement and change. It can denote someone who works in an unstable way – pouring energy into something for a time, and then doing nothing. Of course, self-employed people often work like this from necessity, for their work flow may be variable.

In a more negative sense, the card can refer to someone who cannot sustain energy or effort for long. Boredom, fear of being trapped, or a restless airy mind could all be the culprits here. This individual could still succeed, but needs to accept the fact that he or she requires regular mental stimulus and change.

Theft is another meaning attributed to the seven of Swords. Because it is an airy card, this is more likely to represent the theft of ideas than goods or money. Be cautious about sharing your ideas when you receive this card, or you

Left: The Seven of Pentacles
Middle: The Seven of Swords
Right: The Seven of Cups

cision. You are finding it difficult to act, and may be tormented by an overactive mind filled with negative thoughts. Perhaps some project requires your attention, but you are unable to decide what to do next.

may find a pet project has been taken away from you. Unintentional betrayal, or unconscious tactlessness could also affect your life in some way.

Reversed

Keyword: Superficiality

When the seven of Swords appears in a reversed position, its main message is one of superficiality. This is especially true of the spoken or written word, and thought processes in general. There is something slick, false and insubstantial about conversations, promises or compliments denoted by this card.

Sometimes it indicates a fast-talking person who enjoys the power of words, without considering their true meaning. You are in danger of being manipulated, given faulty advice, or talked into some scheme you may regret later. Do not believe all you hear or read; the seven of Swords reversed is full of tricks and traps for the unwary.

When this card refers to yourself, or an aspect of character it suggests inde-

THE SEVEN OF CUPS

Keywords: All that glisters is not gold

The seven of Cups presents a multitude of possibilities and choices. But, at this stage, none of them is quite real – there are many ifs and buts, doubts and illusions surrounding practical matters. Nothing is seen clearly, although it all sounds wonderful.

When this card appears in a reading it augurs apparent success and abundant opportunity. Yet as soon as you try to pin these things down, they slip and slide away from you. The seven of Cups is sometimes linked to the idea of fairy gold. This mythical substance had a tendency to change form, or disappear altogether when required.

So sit back, and wait and see how things develop, for they may not be exactly as they seem. There is a danger of getting carried away, and scattering your energy in too many directions.

Confusion reigns just now, although something solid and positive could well emerge when the mists clear.

Sometimes this card refers to an emotional choice. There may be several potential partners; you like them all but are not drawn strongly in any one direction. But you feel as if you should make a choice, or perhaps one of them is pressing for a decision. Do not act immediately, your judgment is likely to be unsound at present. Adopt a wait-and-see policy until you feel less confused.

Reversed

Keywords: Dangerous delusions

The dreamy qualities of the seven of Cups are strengthened when it is reversed. But this time there is something negative about the enchantments and fantasies which it denotes. This card warns of deception; you could be deceiving yourself in some way or living in a fantasy world.

Sometimes this card warns against getting lost through drinking too much, taking drugs, or otherwise losing a sense of practical reality. This is an obstacle to overcome if you are to succeed.

If you have recently had some small success, do not rest on your laurels. There is a danger here that you will sit back, imagining future triumphs and forget to work towards them.

In relationships, there may also be a sense of deception and delusion. Uncertainty about emotions, or self-created fantasies may be clouding matters. It is hard to be objective, and no permanent decisions should be taken yet.

THE EIGHTS

Keywords: The balance of power

The number eight is associated with Saturn, and – like four – refers to structures and foundations. However, the eights also incorporate the ideas of change and balance, and the concept of balancing both material and spiritual worlds. It is a strong, energetic, masculine number denoting progress, rather than change for the sake of change.

It is linked with both Strength and Justice in the Major Arcana, depending upon which deck you have – or which system you follow. Curiously, this number relates to both good judgment and strength in numerology, for these are both qualities embodied by the planet Saturn. The eights bring welcome clarity after the confusion inherent in the sevens.

Eight is also traditionally a number of destiny and karma. This means that as you have sown, so shall you reap. Whatever positive effort and energy you have put into your life will return to you, as indeed will anything negative and destructive you have been responsible for. The eights represent these two extremes of power; growth and restriction; gain and sacrifice.

THE EIGHT OF WANDS

Keywords: Fast-expanding horizons

Speed and action are the most important basic meanings of the eight of Wands. When this card appears it indicates that things are opening up in some way. News, letters, and all sorts of communications are highlighted now, and should be bringing changes in their wake. There is great energy in the eight of Wands, and a powerful feeling of expansion. Frequently this card denotes fresh ideas and business expansion. Sometimes it relates to your social life, and suggests that new friends – or perhaps a romantic interest – are about to brighten your days.

This is also one of the cards relating to travel, because it signifies new horizons. Such travel is likely to be educational or career–oriented, rather than simply for rest or pleasure.

Reversed

Keywords: More haste less speed

Trying to get things done in a hurry can often result in mistakes. The eight of Wands reversed warns against sudden decisions or actions, and above all, against committing anything rash to paper.

Sometimes, sudden events outside your control can disrupt the best–laid plans when this card appears. Strikes, demonstrations, or transport disputes could hold you up or slow you down. This is not a good time to try and get somewhere in a hurry. It might be better to rearrange trips, or allow extra time for them if they are essential.

THE EIGHT OF PENTACLES

Keywords: New skills

The eight of Pentacles is an industrious card, primarily relating to work and practical abilities. It often signifies training, apprenticeship, or further education of some kind. It denotes all kinds

of courses, especially those which are taken as part of an existing career or job. Knowledge and skills are being expanded, added to or brushed up in some way.

There may be new machinery at work to master, or further training is required before you can be promoted. Evening classes are sometimes suggested, too – as are all short coursed of a practical nature.

Reversed

Keywords: Problems with work

The eight of Pentacles reversed denotes meaningless toil, and a feeling of limitation at work. Either the work itself is to blame, or you will not learn new skills.

One way or another, there are problems with your working life. You may be in the wrong job, or misusing your talents. Sometimes this misuse has mildly criminal overtones, and refers to cash

Left: The Eight of Wands
Right: The Eight of Pentacles

Left: The Eight of Swords
Right: The Eight of Cups

earned by 'moonlighting' or other unde-clared income. It can denote dishonest business practices and shady deals of various kinds.

Look to the other cards for confir-mation of this meaning, however. Nine times out of ten the eight of Pentacles reversed simply augurs difficulties at work, or even job loss.

THE EIGHT OF SWORDS

Keyword: Bondage

The eight of Swords refers to a period of temporary restriction. Mentally, the querent feels trapped and seems unable to break free. Indeed, he or she is unable to see a solution to problems at the moment and feels very much alone in dealing with difficulties. It is impor-tant to realise that thinking about things in a fresh way encourages the capacity to loosen the bonds.

Usually, a lot of mental energy is going to waste when this card appears.

Indecision, worry, and constant fretting are acting as energy blocks. However, the situation must be faced squarely and some decision arrived at in the near future. It may not be possible to take control immediately, but this is what is required in the long term. Outside help may be needed to put problems in per-spective, or analyse them clearly and unemotionally. Unexpected solutions are possible.

Reversed
Keyword: Release

A restrictive situation or way of thinking is passing out of your life. Renewed confidence and a sense of relaxation enable you to solve prob-lems, and move forward once again. A great deal of hard thinking has preceded this release; it has not come about through luck or circumstance.

When the eight of swords reversed comes in answer to a relationship ques-tion, it suggests a quarrelsome patch and selfish behaviour. One partner may be trying to dominate the other, or generally throwing weight around. This is generally not deliberate, however, but represents an overall thoughtlessness and lack of consideration for others. Other cards will indicate whether this is a passing phase, or signifies deeper problems.

THE EIGHT OF CUPS

Keywords: Moving away

The movement implied by the eight of Cups is primarily emotional. It speaks of a situation or relationship which has been significant. Energy and emotion have been invested during the past, and now the querent is moving away and abandoning what has been achieved.

Sometimes, you realize that a relationship or pet project was not what you thought it was. It lacks substance somehow, and has not brought you the happiness you imagined it would. This meaning also applies to success, which, when it comes seems empty and futile. It is important to realize that, because this is a watery card, these feelings may be subjective. Rejection is accompanied by a feeling of searching for meaning, happiness and contentment.

Part of this search could involve an actual journey, or a period of restless travelling. These trips may eventually provide the answer, although they usually signify an inability to feel settled.

Reversed
Keywords: Fantasy and depression

The eight of Cups reversed denotes a period of emotional confusion. Fantasies are preferred to reality. Depression is close to the surface, and there may be a lack of interest in life. There is a feeling of quiet desperation; it is hard to see the way ahead.

Physically, this represents exhaustion. There is not enough energy to solve all these problems. A failed relationship is often the root cause, or an endless search for perfection in either work or love. Outside help will be needed to halt this destructive phase, for you or the querent are unable to see the wood for the trees at this point.

THE NINES
Keywords: Completion and purification

Nine is the last single number, and as such it represents the end of a cycle. It is a feminine number, signifying love, prosperity, and the positive ability to attract what one needs. It also shows that although much has been achieved, there is still more to learn, or to be faced.

The nines are linked with the Hermit in the Major Arcana, which also carries this meaning. Purification and reassessment are required if life is to go forward in a positive way. It is not enough to rest on one's laurels, basking in self-satisfaction.

The number nine is associated with muses of classical Greek mythology. Originally, there were three muses. They later tripled, and became nine goddesses, each presiding over a different facet of learning and inspiration. Three is frequently associated with goddesses, for many ancient goddesses had three faces. Nine is, therefore, also a number associated with the feminine principle, spiritual love, and the striving for perfection on every level.

THE NINE OF WANDS
Keywords: Strength and prudence

The nine of Wands says 'you've come a long way', and augurs recovery from illness, success and achievement. Efforts have paid off, problems have been overcome, and the goal is in sight. However, there is one last challenge, one last push required before you can relax completely.

When this card appears it signifies reserves of strength. These are available, even if you find it hard to believe. Success will be yours if you can reach deep down inside yourself and use this energy.

When the nine of Wands turns up in the cards of someone who is already successful, it counsels prudence. Most obstacles have been overcome, but it would be wise to remain vigilant in the immediate future.

Psychologically, this card indicates someone who feels threatened, insecure and uncertain inside. Such people may appear successful to others, but have not really accepted this themselves. Perhaps they have had a long fight to get to the top, or realize their dreams, and cannot forget the days when they felt vulnerable to failure. They doubt their own strength, and underestimate their own drive and energy – which is usually considerable.

Reversed

Keywords: Loss of strength

When the nine of Wands appears reversed it denotes loss of strength, usually in the face of yet more obstacles or difficulties. It often indicates past carelessness in health matters, which has contributed to the present situation. Energy is depleted, not only because of making efforts and fighting to achieve something, but also through neglect.

However, success and victory are still possible even when the card is reversed. Delays should be expected, and more attention paid to health. Sometimes this card indicates mental

debility due to overwork. In this instance, some kind of meditation could prove helpful. A programme of physical activity might also provide a useful antidote to mental stress, and give the mind a chance to rest.

THE NINE OF PENTACLES

Keywords: Pleasure and gain

The nine of Pentacles signifies a secure financial plateau. Much has been achieved, and you are now able to enjoy yourself. There is a strong feeling of sustenance, material comfort, and solid sensual pleasure about this card. Money comes easily, and is no longer a worry.

Self-sufficiency is also indicated. You are able to enjoy your success, relish your achievements, and feel complete without the approval of others. There is much pleasure to be gained from improving your home, buying new clothes, and treating yourself well.

Left: The Nine of Wands
Right: The Nine of Pentacles

Somehow, selfishness or self-indulgence do not spoil this picture, for you deserve these rewards.

Sometimes this card points to an earthy love of nature, growing things, and cultivating plants. It can point a career or hobby in these areas which brings happiness and a sense of serenity.

Reversed

Keywords: Financial strictures

When the nine of Pentacles appears reversed it signifies that material security is presently at risk. This can take many forms, and surrounding cards should be consulted for further information. A business may be unable to expand; there is an unexpected drain on material resources – extra expenses, high interest rates, or cancelled orders could all be responsible.

Bad management or risky investments can also be suggested. Present standards of living will be hard to maintain, and some kind of temporary loss is to be expected. Lack of sufficient money may also be making it difficult to expand a business, or improve a property at this time.

THE NINE OF SWORDS

Keywords: Oppression, fear and anxiety

The nine of Swords represents a negative plateau, a dark place full of fear and suffering. This may be the sum total of an extremely difficult time, suggesting an accumulation of stress and worry. There seems to be nowhere to turn, nowhere to hide. Sleep patterns may be disturbed by nightmares, high anxiety, or feelings of some vague danger. Sometimes this card represents real sickness, oppressive neighbours, a painful love relationship, or recent bereavement.

Despair about any of these things has grown into a monster, and seems out of control. There is a negative atmosphere around the querent, which is often not entirely self-created. The reaction to this is, however, that knowledge should not lessen concern for the pain and anguish this person is suffering. It does point to a solution, for these problems must be faced up to, and vanquished.

When this card appears it points to a 'dark night of the soul', and invariably to a complex situation. Occasionally, the suffering inherent in this card has been blown up out of all proportion and simply requires someone sensible to come up with a workable solution. At other times, only time and courage will heal the wounds.

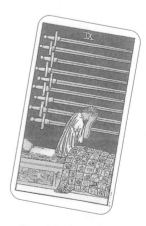

Above: The Nine of Swords

Reversed

Keywords: A light at the end of the tunnel

When the nine of Swords appears reversed it signifies the end of a bad time. Light, hope, strength and faith will triumph. This process will not be easy, for it demands honesty and patience.

Sometimes, this card suggests a revision of old attitudes and behaviour patterns. Some of these things can be discarded now, to make way for new ones. Worry and stress may have been blocking emotion and sensuality for some time. Release from mental fear will restore harmony.

THE NINE OF CUPS

Keywords: Fulfilment and well-being

The nine of Cups is an extremely positive, radiant card. It suggests contentment, physical health, and success. A creative and emotional peak has been reached, your dreams are about to come true, and there is a joyful quality to life.

Emotionally, your relationships are particularly fulfilling. Love flows easily between partners, close family and friends. There is no sense of frustration or lack, and communication with others reaches new and intimate depths.

Creatively, ideas are coming easily and there is plenty of energy to implement them. Something you have wrestled with for a long time may now go smoothly and effortlessly at last.

Reversed

Keywords: Beware of feeling smug

The nine of Cups reversed is a warning against complacency. Everything may be going very well, and there is a danger of becoming lazy and careless.

In relationships, this card suggests that you are taking it all for granted and need to put in a bit more effort. You may feel secure, and think that you can relax completely. Your partner may not see things this way, and could be feeling neglected and resentful. This card often appears after the courtship stage is over and the relationship has been formalized in some way – either through marriage, or living together. Some fresh input is required if the association is to expand and grow.

These meanings also apply to creative endeavours, and business partnerships. Do not let success go to your head, says the nine of Cups, or you may lose everything you have worked so hard to achieve.

Above: The Nine of Cups

Above: 18th-century Florentine Tarot decks

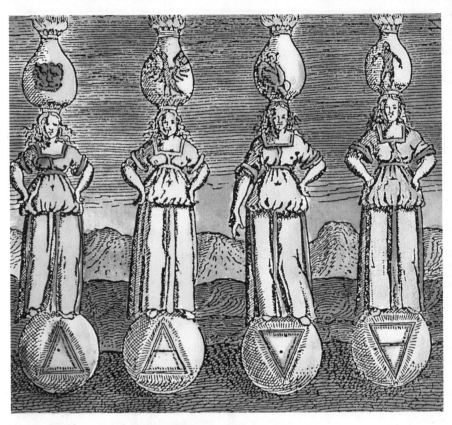

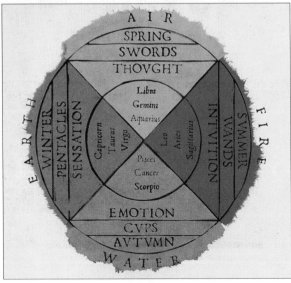

Above: Personifications of the four elements. From left to right: earth, water, air and fire. From the engravings of J.D. Mylius, 1622

Left: The Minor Arcana and the elements

Right: The Rider-Waite deck

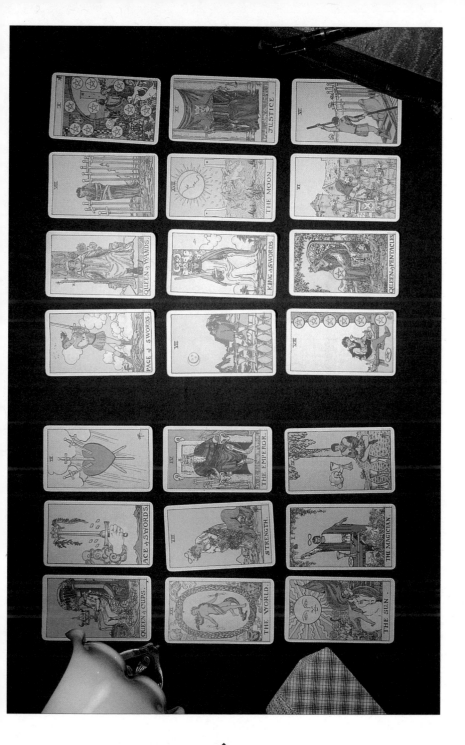

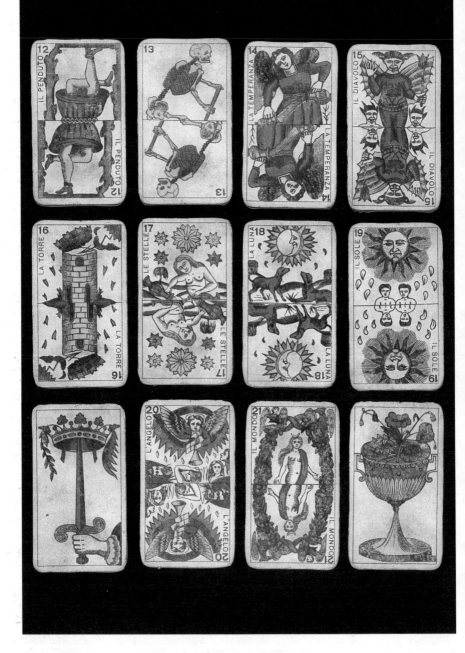

Above: 19th-century Italian tarocchi Tarot cards

Above: A selection of cards from the Marseilles deck

Above: The Four Humours of early medicine were linked to the elements
From top left: phlegmatic *water;* sanguine *air;* choleric *fire;* melancholic *earth*

Above: A 17th-century engraving of the alchemical cosmic vision of the marriage of heaven and earth and of the male and female principles, contained in the Emerad Tablet

Above left: The Ace of Wands from a 17th-century Italian deck. The Ace of Wands suggests expansion and optimism

Above right: The Two of Pentacles, a card associated with a financial, material, or practical balancing act

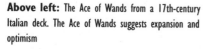

Right: In revolutionary France, pages were out of fashion, so this page was renamed Equality of Wands

THE TENS

Keyword: Transcendence

The tens in the Minor Arcana represent an overview of their suit. In many ways they reflect the Aces, for they are similarly powerful and filled with energy. In numerology, the number ten is usually reduced to one – representing the start of a cycle which finishes with the number nine. The tens of the Tarot are numbers in their own right, standing for transformation, and the consolidation of matters before a new chapter can begin.

Astrologically, each ten contains elements of the quadruplicity (group of three signs) attached to its suit. So the ten of Wands encompasses the fiery energies of Aries, Leo and Sagittarius; ten of Pentacles, Taurus, Virgo and Capricorn; ten of Swords, Gemini, Libra and Aquarius; and ten of Cups, Cancer, Scorpio and Pisces.

Each ten symbolizes the essence of its ruling element, and relevant area of influence. Joyful emotions overflow in the ten of Cups; negative ways of thinking are transformed by the Swords; earthy financial and family matters are the essence of the Pentacles; while the fiery lure of power and success is represented by the ten of Wands.

The tens correspond to the Wheel of Fortune in the Major Arcana, and like this card they suggest that things are shifting and changing in your life. These cards are also – like the Wheel of Fortune – part of a larger pattern. Fate, destiny and karma may be involved when the tens appear, and they often signify groups of people, ideas and events which have gathered together to form a meaningful episode in life.

THE TEN OF WANDS

Keywords: Ambitious burdens

The ten of Wands represents a burden, and because it is a fiery card this burden is connected with power, ambition and success. Winning is important here, not really for the money, but for the ultimate realization of a dream.

Tremendous hard work is usually indicated when this card appears in a spread; at times, it may all seem too much. However, the vitality inherent in this card promises that achievement is possible and, indeed, probable.

Sometimes, this card augurs a period of overwork and obsessive behaviour; the career is seen as all-important. If other cards suggest health or relationship problems it is likely that the overwhelming desire to succeed is proving detrimental to other areas of life. Problems with delegation are very likely, or a fear of losing control of everything that has been gained so far.

Reversed

Keywords: Welcome responsibilities

When the ten of Wands appears reversed it signals the end of a period of very hard work. There is a feeling of expansiveness and generosity towards colleagues, combined with a desire to share both success and responsibility with a group of like-minded people.

Sometimes, the reversed position suggests that you will be promoted, but this time it is welcome responsibility, and does not indicate an onerous burden which must be carried alone.

Left: The Ten of Wands
Right: The Ten of Pentacles

THE TEN OF PENTACLES

Keywords: Finance and the family

The ten of Pentacles is connected with both financial matters and family background. Sometimes this meaning is split in two, at others it clearly suggests money connected with family – such as an inheritance, financial gift, or practical help from the family. A family business could provide employment, a loan, or prove beneficial in other ways.

This meaning will usually be clarified by the appearance of court cards relating to parents, siblings, or other relations. If the card indicates an inheritance, for example, cards relating to legal matters are likely to fall nearby.

Secondly, the ten of Pentacles augurs money, success and material comfort, with a sense of permanence and security. This card often augurs unearned money, rather than salary increases. Tax rebates, and profits on stocks and shares also comes under its aegis.

Reversed

Keywords: Impermanence of wealth and the burdens of tradition

The ten of Pentacles reversed may also be divided into two, distinct, areas of meaning. Family misfortune, or a burdensome family are often suggested by this position.

Family traditions or expectations could be proving difficult to live up to, and you or the querent might feel restricted or inhibited by your background. The question, and surrounding cards should be considered to ascertain whether this meaning is correct. This card would amplify the meaning of the Hierophant, for example, or further illuminate the difficulties suggested by the eight of Swords.

When the ten of Pentacles does not refer to the family, it suggests financial misfortune, reducing potential profits or undermining material security. An inheritance or other lump sum may be delayed – or turn out to be smaller than you had hoped.

THE TEN OF SWORDS

Keywords: The only way is up

Traditionally the card of ruin and betrayal, the ten of Swords is often interpreted as the most doom-laden card in a disruptive suit, but it does have some redeeming features.

Because it is an airy card, the betrayal this card sometimes warns of often takes the form of lies and slander, representing a betrayal of confidence and trust. Be careful in whom you confide, and keep your own counsel when this card appears, especially if other 'gossipy' cards fall nearby – the Page of Swords or the Devil for example. The written word may be source of trouble too, so think twice before signing documents without reading them carefully.

The Ten of Swords also augurs the end of something. This may be a relationship, job, or even a set of beliefs. This ending is often painful, and usually requires great understanding and courage. However, this dark time represents the end of a run of bad luck and things can only get better.

Left: The Ten of Swords
Right: The Ten of Cups

Reversed

Keywords: Negative thinking

When the ten of Swords is reversed it denotes the enemy within. There maybe some brief respite in a troubled period, but difficulties will continue if some effort is not made to overcome negative thought patterns.

Speech often provides useful clues, for people who are very low frequently use pessimistic phrases. They are always on the look-out for trouble, illness, and expect people to treat them badly. This is often a self-fulfilling prophecy, and so their lives are full of problems as result.

THE TEN OF CUPS

Keywords: Lasting spiritual happiness

The ten of Cups represents lasting happiness, dreams come true, and generally conveys a felling of abundant joy.

In relationships it augurs permanence and growth. Valuable friendships are included here, as well as love affairs and family life. The inner satisfaction and self-love of the nine of Cups turns outwards, and strong emotional ties with others are formed. When this card comes in answer to a question, perhaps as a 'result' card, it foretells success; events will work out to your advantage.

Reversed
Keyword: Disruption

The ten of Cups reversed suggests emotional disruption, quarrels and losses. These may be temporary, of course, and other cards should be consulted for more information.

In some circumstances, this card suggests that you may have to move from a much-loved house, town, or even country. At other times, it signifies that you may experience this sense of loss because others move away.

THE COURT CARDS OF WANDS

THE KING OF WANDS

Keywords: Drive and integrity

The King of Wands often represents an energetic, vital man whom you are likely to encounter at work, or through business connections. He is a strong character, with a good sense of humour and is usually excellent company. In business, he is fair-minded and works hard for his often considerable success. As a colleague or partner he is full of ideas, with the drive to back them up.

In his private life, he is generous, romantic and trustworthy. His fondness for the countryside leads him to live there, especially in later life, for he loves to spend time in the open air. Despite these sterling characteristics, the King of Wands sometimes indicates the male partner in an illicit love affair. When other cards, such as the Lovers reversed suggest this, he will be charming and fun to be with – but ultimately unavailable. If you fall in love with him in these circumstances, you are certain to be playing with fire.

Reversed

Keywords: Selfish and freedom-loving

The King of Wands reversed may reveal an unpleasant character. His views are narrow, and he is often selfish, and intolerant. He is ambitious, and full of drive; little will stop him on his road to the top. In business matters this man is not to be trusted, and he could be using you to further his own ends.

In relationships he suggests someone who is lively and interesting. This attractive man makes a marvellous companion – in the short term. Do not raise your hopes, or make wedding plans, for he loves his freedom and is not ready to take love seriously. Enjoy it while it lasts.

Abstract

Keywords: Negotiations and agreements

When the King of Wands signifies abstract concepts the card can indicate a marriage which involves some kind of property settlement, or formal financial agreement. It may also suggest a legacy; business wheeling and dealing; all types of negotiations; plus bodies such as trusts, charities, and philanthropic organizations. Other cards will confirm these meanings.

THE QUEEN OF WANDS

Keywords: Warm, light and loyal

The Queen of Wands is an independent, charismatic woman. She makes a great friend, since she is generous, hospitable, and good company. She is always full of bright ideas, and can be very helpful to those she loves. Once she has taken you into her life, she is loyal and often inspiring for she is a positive thinker.

In love, she is passionate and sensual. She brings a sense of humour to her relationships, and is rarely bad-tempered for long. She loves to have fun, and enjoys lively company. She needs admiration and reassurance in a relationship, for deep down she lacks confidence and hates to be taken for granted. Possessive behaviour frightens her, and may drive her away eventually.

Reversed

Keywords: Unreliable and unstable

When the Queen of Wands is reversed she often indicates an unreliable friend or colleague. Such a person may have made promises he or she has no intention of honouring, so do not take too much on trust. If other cards augur serious trouble, then she stands for a jealous and vengeful woman. This unstable person enjoys stirring things up, and can take offence where none was intended. Keep her at arm's length, or she will attempt to take over your life.

Abstract

Keywords: Rural pleasures, success for women

When signifying abstract concepts, the Queen of Wands denotes rural pleasures and the countryside in general. She can also augur business success for women, and raising money for charity.

THE KNIGHT/PRINCE OF WANDS

Keywords: Impetuous energy

The impetuous Knight of Wands represents a gregarious, intelligent young man. This character has great plans for the future, and with his energy and creativity he will eventually succeed. However, at this stage in his life he has little staying power, is easily bored by the daily grind, and better at starting projects than following them through.

Sometimes this card can indicate an older man who has a very boyish character and attitude to life. In this case, he is less attractive for emotionally he is looking for a mother-figure, and in business he is flighty.

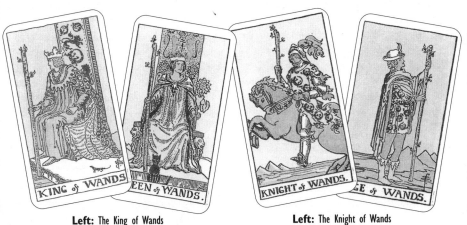

Left: The King of Wands
Right: The Queen of Wands

Left: The Knight of Wands
Right: The Page of Wands

Reversed

Keyword: Untrustworthy

The Knight of Wands reversed is a fast-talking, charming rogue. He is not to be trusted in any way, but can be hard to resist.

Abstract

Keyword: Activity

The Knight of Wands denotes movement and activity in your life. Visitors, short trips, and places are all indicated. This card sometimes ushers in a phase when you receive lots of letters, phone calls, and potential job offers. Socially, you won't be short of invitations.

THE PAGE/PRINCESS OF WANDS

Keywords: Feeling more creative

The Page of Wands represents a lively, intelligent child or teenager of either sex. More frequently, this card suggests the dawning of creativity and an upsurge of energy. It is a positive influence, bringing similar activity to the Knight – but to a lesser degree. You may expect short journeys, invitations, and plenty of lively conversation. This card also bodes well for property matters.

Reversed

Keywords: Disrupted communication

Hyperactivity, reading and writing difficulties, and general instability affecting a young child or adolescent are suggested here.

THE COURT CARDS OF PENTACLES

THE KING OF PENTACLES

Keywords: Sensual, solid and financially secure

The King of Pentacles represents a responsible, cautious individual. This man has an excellent head for business, although he is certainly not a born speculator. His patience pays off instead, for he has the foresight to plan carefully ahead. Since material security is important to him, he has usually got something tucked away 'for a rainy day', and is often well-off – or even wealthy.

In relationships he is reliable and loyal, once he has made his mind up about you as a friend or lover – often a slow process. He is sensual, and loves the good things in life. His innate conservatism means that he generally prefers traditional surroundings, and well-made things for he knows these have stood the test of time. He can be possessive of both friends and lovers, but this must be balanced against his depth of feeling and need for security. His company may not stimulate or sparkle, but it is soothing and steadfast.

Reversed

Keywords: A Stick-in-the-mud

A reversed King of Pentacles indicates a miserly, boring character. He can be an obstinate bully who cannot or will not see reason. In love, his possessiveness and jealousy may ruin the relationship. In business his inability to take even the smallest risk can lead to his downfall, for he is unable to take advantage of opportunities.

Abstract

Keywords: Gradual material improvement

When signifying an abstract meaning, the King of Pentacles augurs financial improvement, promotion, and the gradual establishment of a profession or business.

It can stand for large companies, and well-established organizations – especially those connected with the professions, property, or banking. If negatively aspected, probable business failure is suggested, as are insufficient capital or a delay concerning a loan.

Left: The King of Pentacles
Right: The Queen of Pentacles

THE QUEEN OF PENTACLES

Keywords: Supportive, practical, and kind

The Queen of Pentacles represents a warm-hearted woman, who is fond of luxury, food, good clothes and elegant places. She often has an instinct for history, and is drawn to antiques and old buildings.

As a friend she can provide practical support in a crisis. As a lover she is sensual, kind, and loving – but requires a financially-stable partner. She dislikes very noisy surroundings, failure, and has a strong aversion to poverty.

In business she is often very successful, and has a good understanding of management, budgeting and organization. She works hard, and will tolerate

Left: The Knight of Pentacles
Right: The Page of Pentacles

boring activities if they are likely to lead to something better.

Reversed

Keywords: Greed and ambition

The Queen of Pentacles reversed is extremely selfish and hard-hearted. She can be greedy about food, money, or material possessions, spending lavishly on herself with little thought for others. She can be a gold-digger who marries for money.

In business she presents an over-ambitious woman, with a good head for money and future planning. However, her work leaves little time for her to enjoy love or friendship since she values a healthy bank-balance more highly. She only cultivates people if they are useful to her, or can help her achieve her ambitions.

Abstract

Keywords: Rewards and treats

As an abstract card, the Queen of Pentacles indicates a desire to enjoy and acquire beautiful material things. Sometimes this card appears in the middle of a period of very hard work, and suggests a need to reward yourself with a few indulgent treats such as holidays, jewellery, or other luxuries. For women, it can denote beauty treatments, massage, new clothes or a big bottle of expensive scent.

When negative, the Queen of Pentacles may hint at a very selfish attitude towards money. There may be a tendency to spend on yourself and forget

to share success with friends and lovers.

THE KNIGHT/PRINCE OF PENTACLES

Keywords: Ambition and determination

The Knight of Pentacles may be just starting out in life, yet his determined brand of ambition will eventually propel him to the top. He is hard-working, patient and rather conventional. At times he may seem slow, and a little dull, for his earthy mind can lack imagination. However, he is usually honest and forthright and makes a loyal friend or business partner who will not throw in the towel at the first hurdle.

Reversed

Keywords: Practical limitations

The Knight of Pentacles reversed augurs financial strictures, career problems, and difficulties with work in general. It can stand for a poor man, whose confidence is as depleted as his bank-balance.

Abstract

Keywords: Taking steps towards security

As an abstract card, the Knight of Pentacles denotes the dawning of ambition, and with it the ability to work hard and tenaciously towards a goal. Money may not be exactly abundant, but with a firm aim in sight future rewards are more than likely.

This card can also stand for savings, loans, and investors. If negative, it suggests over-extended credit, refusal of loans or mortgages, and a sensation of running on the spot financially.

THE PAGE/PRINCESS OF PENTACLES

Keywords: Minor financial improvement, happy news

When representing a child, the Page or Princess of Pentacles suggests a steady, good-natured personality. This person is unimaginative, careful, and loving. There may be weight problems, or a very sweet tooth.

Abstract

Keywords: Small gains and losses

As an abstract card the Page of Pentacles signifies news about money or minor property matters. There could be small financial improvements, such as a minor rise in salary or some interest on investments.

There is good news connected with family, close friends or children.

Negatively, money could be rather tight just now. Also, this card may act as a warning against the theft of a purse, wallet or handbag. There could be unexpected bills to pay, too.

Reversed

Keywords: Nascent introversion

Introverted children, who have noticeable difficulties in mixing with others, can be indicated by this card. There may be problems with shyness, or the child could be non-communicative and moody.

THE COURT CARDS OF SWORDS

THE KING OF SWORDS

Keywords: Logical, clever and quick-witted

The King of Swords represents a clever, well-educated man with a particular gift for logical argument, and rational thought. He often stands for a lawyer, accountant, doctor or psychologist. Nine times out of ten you will find him working in some professional capacity, where his bright and restless mind can be put to good use.

In matters of love, the King of Swords can be a little chilly and lacking in substance. He is uncomfortable with messy, dark and primitive emotions – finding them unacceptable in himself and embarrassing in others. He usually feels emotion, but has great difficulty in expressing it – his key phrase is 'I think', rather than 'I feel'.

He is an entertaining companion, however, and often a charming flirt. He requires lots of mental stimulation from friends and lovers, and is also likely to enjoy games which entail some kind of mental challenge. Crossword puzzles, chess, and card games can all help him burn off surplus mental energy.

Reversed

Keywords: Malice and manipulation

The King of Swords reversed indicates a difficult character who is likely to make destructive use of words. Such a man will happily play 'devil's advocate' in

Left: The King of Swords
Right: The Queen of Swords

arguments, and is often adept at manipulative mind games. This position can suggest a silver-tongued liar who is able to run rings around slower, more trusting types.

At his worst, the King of Swords reversed indicates an intelligent but malicious man who could be making trouble for you. He is capable of generating written libel or spoken slander, or drafting documents such as contracts full of traps for the unwary.

Abstract
Keyword: Advice

As an abstract card, the King of Swords stands for good, clear advice. This can be about work, or refer to legal matters – depending upon surrounding cards.

THE QUEEN OF SWORDS
Keywords: Cool, charming and intelligent

The Queen of Swords represents an intelligent, perceptive woman. Like her masculine counterpart, she is rational and logical. In all but the most extreme situations her heart is firmly ruled by her cool, quick-witted head.

She loves a lively social life, needing the stimulation of other people's ideas and enjoying wide-ranging conversation. Her friendships are rarely deep, for she prefers to skim the surface and enjoys variety. When she does form a lasting attachment, however, she is very loyal and can prove to be strong and clear-headed in a crisis.

In love, the Queen of Swords is idealistic and shys away from possessive or

Left: The Knight of Swords
Right: The Page of Swords

over-emotional types. She is a firm believer in sexual equality, and likes to talk about problems. She is also graceful, and her physical movements are usually deft and economical – making her an excellent dancer. There is often a fondness for music, too, especially in romantic situations.

Of all the Queens, she is the most likely to represent an unavailable woman with whom you or the querent are having an affair. She is not particularly interested in sex for its own sake, but can sometimes enjoy the deceptive and flirtatious aspects of an illicit liaison.

Reversed

Keywords: A dangerous gossip, lonely and bitter

The Queen of Swords reversed represents an enemy who is secretly spreading gossip about you. In this position she suggests a troublesome woman who may be motivated by jealousy or sheer spite. She can be dangerous, for she is clever. This position can also indicate a woman who has an unhappy emotional life. She can simply represent a divorcee or widow, or suggest a miserable woman who is bitter about men, sex and love in general.

Abstract

Keywords: A battle of wits

As an abstract card, the Queen of Swords denotes some kind of battle of wits. This can be positive and challenging, or painful and negative depending upon other cards in your spread.

It augurs success in all creative, mental pursuits – such as public speaking, writing, and music. It is also considered a good influence in matters connected with publishing, exams, and any kind of study.

If it is negatively placed, it warns of jealousy in general. Women are particularly unhelpful to you at this time, and could be talking behind your back.

THE KNIGHT/PRINCE OF SWORDS

Keywords: Quick thinking and new ideas

The Knight of Swords represents a confident, articulate young man with blossoming reasoning powers and a subtle wit. Physically restless, he acts quickly, and sometimes impetuously.

This card may represent a student. If working, the Knight of Swords can symbolize people who work in public relations; the media in general; advertising or the music industry.

Reversed

Keyword: Deceit

When the Knight of Swords is reversed he is secretive and treacherous. He may, like the King, tell clever lies; steal your best ideas for his own ends; or provoke quarrels. He can be sly and deceitful, beneath a misleading veneer of honesty.

Abstract

Keywords: Speed and change

As an abstract card, the Knight of Swords rushes in to a spread like a powerful gust of autumn wind. This symbolic blast of fresh air may sweep through your life, bringing sudden change.

There is a strong feeling of surprise which pervades information you receive at this time; whether letters, phone calls, or encounters. An old friend or lover with whom you have lost touch could suddenly reappear in your life. Look to surrounding cards to see which area is most affected by this unexpected surge of energy.

THE PAGE/PRINCESS OF SWORDS

Keywords: The awakening mind

The Page or Princess of Swords denotes a well co-ordinated, bright young person who enjoys games and sports. Generally this card signifies news and communications, contracts and documents, new plans, and minor alterations to documents. It also suggests enjoyable gossip and scandal, pleasure in words, and the awakening or sharpening of the mental faculties.

Reversed

Keyword: Spite

When reversed or ill-aspected, the Page of Swords indicates spiteful gossip, hurtful letters, and a tricksy childish influence. It can also denote lies, white and grey.

THE COURT CARDS OF CUPS

THE KING OF CUPS

Keywords: Imaginative, emotional, charismatic

The imaginative King of Cups represents the most feminine of the four kings. He is usually highly intuitive, and often found in creative jobs or industries. Even in more conventional careers he can be eccentric, making decisions and investments because he 'feels' they are right rather than for any logical reason. These hunches may lead him to become very successful.

His presence is often powerfully charismatic; many people find him magnetic yet difficult. He makes a dangerous enemy, rarely forgetting a betrayal or slight and able to wait for revenge.

In love, he is highly-sexed and emotional. His sensitivity is both a blessing and a curse. On the one hand he can be kind and thoughtful, on the other he imagines insults where none were intended. He can also be very moody and prone to fits of jealousy. However, he is rarely boring or predictable.

Reversed

Keywords: Depressive, escapist, unfaithful

The King of Cups reversed displays escapist tendencies such as heavy drinking, unreliability, or even drug-taking. He can be emotionally repressed, finding it almost impossible to articulate his needs and feelings – or considering them weak and unmanly.

Left: The King of Cups
Right: The Queen of Cups

Left: The Knight of Cups
Right: The Page of Cups

Consequently, he can be prone to depression.

Like the King of Wands, he can indicate an unfaithful partner. But there is big difference between them; the King of Cups is so emotional, and easily-led sexually, that he may give both partners the impression he is passionately in love with them. And this could be true. However, unlike the flirtatious King of Wands, this man is unable to conduct a light, friendly association. As he gets into deeper and deeper waters he finds it hard to know what he wants any more, and eventually drowns in a sea of emotion. Unlucky partners may go down with him.

Abstract

Keywords: Cultural and spiritual activities

As an abstract card, the King of Cups denotes a wide range of artistic and cultural activities. These include individual creative effort; art galleries; publishing; the music industries – both popular and classical; and any aspect of business where these things are important.

In addition, he can stand for 'New Age' businesses and movements associated with alternative or spiritual ideals. Secret organizations may also be suggested, especially those with occult overtones.

THE QUEEN OF CUPS

Keywords: Feminine, artistic spiritual

The Queen of Cups signifies an extremely feminine woman. She is artistic, often psychic, and is highly imaginative. There may be mediumistic abilities, or an inclination towards witchcraft and magic. She has good colour sense, and often wears unusual and individual clothes. Her undoubted talents may be underused, for she tends to be a bit lazy and also lacks confidence.

In love she is sympathetic and very loving. She may have trouble asserting herself, and always puts her man first.

She is prone to bursting into tears, and is very tender-hearted towards weaker souls, those in distress and small animals. She can be delightfully vague, and often has trouble being on time for rendezvous.

Reversed

Keywords: Emotional blocks and changeable moods

The Queen of Cups reversed reveals a changeable, over-emotional woman who can also be manipulative. Her moods make life difficult for lovers, colleagues and friends and she may represent an 'emotional vampire' who drains others of energy.

Sometimes, this position signifies a woman who has sustained painful emotional wounds. She may be locked into an unhappy and unfulfilling relationship, or trapped in a dead-end career. Her talents lie dormant; although she instinctively knows they are there and should be used she does not know how to bring this about.

Abstract

Keywords: Positive fantasy

As an abstract card, the Queen of Cups suggests the world of fantasy and fiction. This may be expressed through books and plays, or in films and pictures. She can represent all kinds of emotional therapy, family therapy and marriage guidance. When negative, this card may indicate repressed emotions, blocked sexuality, self-pity, and emotional exhaustion.

THE KNIGHT/PRINCE OF CUPS

Keywords: Loving, creative, dreamer

The Knight of Cups is sometimes linked to the legendary Grail Knight, who rides off in search of an enlightened ideal. He most often signifies that a lover is on the way, or has just entered someone's life. Here, love is elevated and romantic – reality and familiarity have yet to intrude upon this shining dream.

When indicating a person, the Knight of Cups is usually a spiritual, emotional young man. He is sensitive, artistic or musical, and has high ideals.

Reversed

Keywords: Emotional problems

The Knight of Cups reversed suggests a talented young man who lacks motivation, and may have emotional problems. He is a rather lost, often seeking advice but rarely able to follow it through. He is also likely to be lazy, preferring to sleep and read rather than act and find his fantasies do not live up to reality.

Abstract

Keywords: Developing creativity/spirituality

As an abstract card, the Knight of Cups stands for blossoming or nascent creativity, and a developing interest in spiritual concerns.

It can also refer to classes and groups where holistic or paranormal interests are pursued. These include yoga, psychic development, and meditation. When negative, the Knight of Cups can stand for drugs and drug dealers; and relationships which are not what they seem. Sometimes, it indicates that a lover is leaving.

THE PAGE/PRINCESS OF CUPS

Keywords: Increased intuition

When the Page or Princess of Cups stands for a person, it signifies a gentle and imaginative child, or adolescent, who is sensitive and loving. There may be imaginary fears or emotional difficulties if other cards suggest this.

It can also augur the dawning of creative or intuitive impulses. These interests are likely to be expressed through dreams, reading about unexplained mysteries, and an increased awareness of atmosphere and emotion. You may come into contact with these subjects through friends, or at work – but however they find their way into your life, pay attention, for they are waking up within you. The Page of Cups may also signal some happy emotional news. A friend or relation may fall in love, there may be news of a wedding or engagement, or even a baby.

Reversed

Keyword: Mirage

When reversed, this card suggests an air of unreality, and a lack of coherent action or thought. You, or someone close, may be suffering from bad dreams or nebulous intuitions which are difficult to comprehend.

COMBINATIONS

Sometimes a single spread may contain a combination of numbered cards of the same value. For example, there might be two Aces side by side, or a cluster of court cards. These combinations suggest overall influences or meanings which should be considered in addition to their usual significance. This is particularly true when the cards appear either together, or separated by one other card.

In large spreads you are almost certain to get at least two of a kind appearing somewhere. Such combinations are then only significant if they fall together. In smaller spreads, using approximately five to twenty-one cards, it is worth looking out for them, for they can prove helpful.

ACES

Four Aces: An important, possibly dangerous time. There is great energy here, which may be turned to positive or negative account.

Three Aces: Good news is on the way. Other cards should indicate whether this pertains to career, love, money, or intellectual matters. Success and abundance.

Two Aces: Union, partnership – especially if the Ace of Cups and the Ace of Pentacles fall together. Can also indicate a new home or place of work.

TWOS

Four twos: Groups. Either working groups or teams, or social groups.
Three twos: Reassessment, reshuffles.

THREES

Four threes: Creative productivity, tenacity.
Three threes: Lies, things not as they seem.

FOURS

Four fours: Security, contentment, a welcome rest.
Three fours: Work.

FIVES

Four fives: Competitive influences; unstable partnerships.
Three fives: A solid routine, regular cycles.

SIXES

Four sixes: Harmony.
Three sixes: Completion, attainment.

SEVENS

Four sevens: Intrigue, pitfalls, disappointment.
Three sevens: A happy result of some kind.
Two sevens: Mutual love, or balanced forces.

EIGHTS

Four eights: Activity, journeys, news about work.
Three eights: News of a marriage or other important alliance.
Two eights: Surprise developments.

NINES

Four nines: Accomplishment.
Three nines: Health, wealth and happiness.
Two nines: Documents, usually relating to business matters.

TENS

Four tens: Rather overwhelming success, accompanied by tension. If any are reversed, this is delayed or there are obstacles to overcome.

Three tens: Litigation, business correspondence.
Two tens: Possibility of a new job, lucky breaks.

PAGES

Four: Groups of young people or students. Places where such people gather such as schools, universities.
Three: Parties, fun, lively and/or noisy social events.
Two: Trouble through friends.

KNIGHTS

Four: Action; the male force.
Three: More 'adult' parties than indicated by the pages. Dinners, theatre, small convivial groups.
Two: Meeting old friends.

QUEENS

Four: Entertainment. If any are found reversed, the event may be spoilt.
Three: Female groups or gatherings. Supportive, helpful associations.
Two: Gossip, secrets between friends. Can indicate a rival, or petty betrayal especially if surrounding cards confirm this, or if the cards are reversed.

KINGS

Four: Worldly, public honours; powerful gatherings; important and successful business or political matters.
Three: Groups of men; powerful or influential friendships.
Two: A business partnership; enterprise; co-operation in business affairs.

READING THE TAROT

Before you begin the exciting process of reading Tarot cards, it is important to familiarize yourself as fully as possible with the cards and their meanings. This is a process to be undertaken in a spirit of adventure – with an open mind, a desire to learn more about yourself and others and a childlike sense of fun.

◆ ◆ ◆

Choosing your deck

The first step in learning to read Tarot is to acquire a suitable deck. There are now so many designs available that there is certain to be one which appeals to your taste and cultural background.

This seems to me to be very important, for there is no point working with a deck you don't enjoy using, or can't relate to. You will find it difficult, or even impossible, to understand your cards on any but a dry intellectual level, and your readings will reflect this.

However, some decks do contain richer symbolism than others and are ultimately more satisfying to use for this reason. As you learn more, and become familiar with these aspects of Tarot you will find such decks helpful and inspiring.

Two of the most 'classic' decks to start with are the Marseilles* with its clear medieval images, and the Waite deck with its helpfully-designed Minor

Arcana – each card is pictorial and contains useful clues to the meaning of the numbered suits. Of the many modern decks, the Prediction Tarot contains a realistically-designed Major Arcana that is evocative and easy to use.

But do remember that Tarot reading is an extremely intuitive affair. While there are basic rules and guidelines, it is vital not to get lost in a maze of esoteric dogma. So choose the deck which 'speaks' to you, and stick with that until you feel at home with your cards.

Getting to know the Tarot

Learning the individual meanings of 78 cards, and how they influence each other in a spread is hard work. But it is exciting, illuminating and rewarding as well. The Tarot can act as a key which opens up your intuition, leads to greater self-awareness, and eventually helps you glimpse the vibrant underlying pattern which connects every living

* This is the deck included with your book

thing in the Universe.

You can use the cards for straightforward fortune-telling – which is usually not straightforward at all; for meditation; and for general guidance. The Tarot is very useful when you are trying to sort out all the different factors in a given situation, for it can reveal half-hidden motives and influences outside your immediate awareness or control.

Getting to know your Tarot cards should be undertaken in the spirit of adventure best personified by the Fool, who opens the gateway to the Major Arcana. You will need an open mind; a desire to learn more about the cards, yourself, and others; and a childlike sense of fun and wonder.

Simple exercises

Before getting down to serious study, it is a good idea to familiarize yourself with your chosen deck as a whole. Take out your cards, look at them, handle them, mix them up and put them back in the right order again. Enjoy them.

The next step is to see what they say to you personally, and how you react to each image. Get a fresh notebook specially for the purpose, and gradually work your way through the Major Arcana, card by card. Look carefully at each image, and without referring to any given set of meanings, note down what you think and how you feel about each picture.

You may like to sleep with each card in turn. This is an old method for tuning in to the Tarot, and is valuable if you tend to have vivid and memorable dreams.

Take your chosen card, and have a good look at it before you settle down for the night. You can tuck it under your pillow, or place it on a bedside table. Then ask your subconscious to send you a clear dream about the meaning of the card, which you will remember next day.

When you wake up, try to scribble down your dream pictures as quickly as you can. If there are none, write down how you feel – elated, depressed, calm, or whatever, or any colour which seems to be lingering on your inner screen.

Keep these notes with any others you have made about the card in question; they may seem like gibberish at first but will probably make sense to you later on. These exercises are designed to help you tune in to the Tarot, and gain a sense of it as an entity before you begin delving deeper into each card, its variable meanings and mysterious symbols.

Learning the Tarot alphabet

As a beginner, it is best to approach learning about the Tarot in a gentle way. Do not try to rush it, or take in too much detail at once. You will only get 'occult indigestion'! Read one or two books you understand and enjoy, and then start laying out the cards in simple spreads.

You can read these spreads with the aid of a book (or books) which set out the basic meanings of each card. Do not try to read the cards for anyone else at this point, you might make dangerous mistakes or give misleading advice to an impressionable person.

Do a little sketch of each spread you lay out, and write down what cards appear, their position (either upright or reversed), and where they fall in the spread. Note down the meanings of each card. Sometimes an obvious theme will emerge, at others the spread may seem impenetrable and obscure. Do not fret over these, just note them down with the date and question – if any – and go back to them later on.

You can consult the cards on your own behalf, or ask about other people whom you know. You can even experiment with broader issues, and do spreads about political or business matters in the news. Bear in mind that you are learning all the time, and gradually becoming familiar with your cards. Use your imagination, and do whatever appeals to you.

Story telling

You can also use the cards to tell stories. This is a good way to develop your intuition, and learn how to weave the separate images into a coherent whole. Lay out your cards in a circular or linear pattern – the Horoscope Spread or Twenty–One Card Spread are good ones to choose (see pages 152–154 and 150–151).

Now look at the pattern, and pick out the characters who are going to enact this little drama. These will be court cards (King, Queen, Knight, and Page/Princess), plus any of the Major Arcana cards resembling people –

Empress, Emperor, Fool, High Priestess and so on.

Starting at the beginning of your spread, describe the character who first appears and the kind of situation he or she is in. Moving along the cards, look at the other characters involved and try to imagine the part they are playing. What is affecting them and their behaviour? What is the general mood of the story? Is it a love story, full of Cups; an action story, with plenty of Wands; or is it a deeply symbolic psychological tale, heavily populated with images from the Major Arcana?

Using the Horoscope Spread as an example, you would look first at the overall pattern – and then at the thirteenth card which falls in the middle. This card will either suggest a character, or a situation.

Start with this information, and then proceed around the circle looking at the specific areas of life each position refers to. If you like, you can choose any one of the personalized cards in the deck, and use it as the significator for your story.

Let's say you chose the Emperor, and placed him in the centre of your practice spread: your story will be about a strong, probably successful, and somewhat authoritarian man. Try and picture his age and appearance, imagine his clothes, colouring and so on.

Now, look at the card which you have placed in position 1. This tells you more about the man's character, and will probably reveal any immediate problems too.

Position 2 tells you whether this

Emperor is thriving financially, or whether his imaginary kingdom is going through hard times. Position 3 indicates what news may be expected, and whether or not our character is going to be travelling anywhere. You can proceed like this around the circle, building up a picture of the Emperor and his concerns as you go.

You can either write down your story, or use a little tape recorder and talk your way through. Refer to a convenient list of meanings to help you when you get stuck, but try not to rely too heavily on this information. Story telling is an exercise which is designed to encourage imagination and intuition – essential abilities for any Tarot reader.

DEVELOPING YOUR INTUITION

Intuition plays an important part in successful Tarot reading. A sound working knowledge of the cards is essential, of course, but intuition can make the difference between a good reading and an inspired one.

Many people mistakenly believe they are not 'psychic' or intuitive. They see it as some kind of rare gift or talent which they can never hope to acquire. Astonishing psychic powers may fall into this category – we are not all destined to become great mediums or world-famous healers. But basic extrasensory perception, intuition – or whatever you want to call it – is available to everyone who is prepared to put aside a little time each day, and work towards developing it.

Our intuition seems to be a sixth sense which is often dormant through lack of exercise. But that does not mean it isn't there. We are taught to think in a logical, linear way at school; any further education serves to emphasize structured ways of thinking and presenting arguments. These skills have their place in life, for without them we would be very woolly-minded indeed. Sadly, many of us never realize that we can use our minds in other ways too.

Developing your intuition can help to unlock your creativity, and improve your ability to solve problems. Intuition can be used alongside logical ways of thinking, or provide an inspired overview of a situation. Reading the Tarot requires both kinds of approach. You begin a reading by assessing the cards, looking at the pattern, and checking on the elements represented by the Minor Arcana. Then you try to blend all these disparate pieces of information into a coherent whole. That's where intuition comes in.

So, how do you begin? The first step is to have faith in yourself, and believe that you can develop psychic abilities. Your biggest challenge here is to free yourself from the limiting belief that you are not that kind of person. You can be, if you relax, and adopt a positive attitude.

Secondly, you must make some effort towards developing your psychic abilities. Sometimes learning the Tarot can stimulate these faculties, probably because it is visual and symbolic. Tarot images seem to belong to the universal language of dreams; they may puzzle the conscious mind, but make complete sense on deeper, subconscious levels. Learn to trust your instinctive feelings and reactions to the cards, and eventually you will be able to combine this with what you have consciously learned about them.

One of the first things you can do to encourage your psychic awareness is to pay more attention to your five senses. How often do we really 'see' all the shapes and colours around us? The world is full of beauty and colour, even on the darkest winter day but we rarely notice such subtleties. Just look at a paint chart, and you will realize how many shades of white there are – let alone more obvious colour distinctions.

Hearing is another sense which we usually 'edit' in everyday life, although our brains are busily recording and interpreting every sound we hear. Touch, too, is taken for granted much of the time – while taste and smell are probably the most neglected senses of all. Yet certain smells, for example, have the power to unleash a stream of vivid memories if they are linked to events in our pasts. Other scents can stimulate emotions, uplift or depress us.

By learning to tune into the world around you, and become truly aware of it, you will automatically become more intuitive. Take a little time each day to sit quietly, relax, and become acutely conscious of the messages your five senses are receiving.

Concentrate your attention on them one by one; listen to your heartbeat and breathing, and do not strain or try too hard at first. Just spend ten to fifteen minutes in this kind of contemplation each day, and you will soon become aware of your own inner voice – which is the first step towards becoming more psychic.

There are some excellent books available on psychic development which cover this vast subject in more detail than is possible here. However, here are some basic guidelines.

Learn how to relax, and let go of everyday concerns.

Pay attention to your senses; become intensely aware of the world about you, and listen to what your body is telling you.

Trust your intuition, and believe in it. If your inner voice or sense seems to be telling you something that is not logical, or seems ridiculous, do not dismiss it or try to suppress it. Yes, you could be wrong – but what if you are right?

Remember, pleasure and laughter can be powerful tools in unlocking your intuitive faculties. If you are not enjoying your studies, you will find it much more difficult to learn. And a gentle sense of humour can help to liberate the imaginative child within you, the wise, trusting Fool of the Major Arcana.

THE SPREADS AND HOW TO READ THEM

Choosing your spread

Reading the Tarot can be made a good deal easier by choosing the right spread for your purposes. It is a good idea to hold your chosen pattern in mind while shuffling the cards – or whilst your querent is doing so.

Your deck is a tool, which if wisely used will shed some light upon problems or provide an answer to a question. But you must learn to programme this tool correctly, and not expect any old pattern to prove clear and accurate.

The types of spread

Basically, spreads divide into three broad types. There are the general-purpose 'Past, Present and Future' varieties, which provide a broad time framework for prediction. Then there are those which are designed to analyse a single, specific, question, such as the Celtic Cross or the Horseshoe layouts. In addition, some spreads – such as the Horoscope or Tree of Life – can be used to provide an overall look at the various areas of someone's life. The individual positions of the cards in both layouts are designed to answer a question and those that take a look at various areas of life are very important. Each position carries its own meaning, and whatever card falls there must be interpreted in the context of this meaning.

Spreads such as the Horoscope are often useful to begin with, for they will give you a good idea of what is, has been, and will be important to your inquirer. These spreads can help you tune in to each other, too, so that you both relax and the reading has a chance to flow. Sometimes, a general spread will be all that is required to settle someone's mind.

Specific problems

However, when there are difficulties in one particular area – or areas if your inquirer is really going through a bad time – then a specific spread is called for. It can be helpful to take a close look at the inquirer – or, indeed, at yourself – with a general spread, and then go on to try and answer a definite, clearly-framed question relating to the problem.

Always take one problem at a time. If someone has a rocky love-life and is also in financial difficulties these two questions must be separated, and dealt with accordingly. The general spread should have indicated which problem seemed to be the most pressing, and whether the two were connected in reality or only in the querent's mind.

For example, someone could be experiencing relationship problems as a result of one partner being out of work. Finances would then be stretched, since only one income would be coming in. Such an imbalance might then lead to psychological problems for both partners, resulting in a difficult relationship. On the other hand, someone could be so worried about money, perhaps unneccessarily, that tension and inability to enjoy love and friendship to the full result.

Timing

Finally, there is the elusive question of timing. This is notoriously difficult to get right, for in many ways the Tarot affords a glimpse into a timeless zone. This nebulous dreamlike world appears to be much affected by what kind of person you, or your querent, are.

Some people seem to gallop through lives filled with constant drama and change, while others spend year after year wondering when something interesting will happen. These extremes may also be found in a short period, such as a year. Some months pass peacefully, while others are packed with events and meetings.

Most people instinctively know that, whatever the calendar or clock may say, time can fly by or drag its heels, seeming to obey its own laws. In many readings, time appears to be an elastic substance that defies an absolute definition. Interestingly, a number of physicists, including Stephen Hawking, author of the best-seller *A Brief History of Time*, are now arriving at the same conclusion.

Spreads such as the Twelve Month or Calendar spread can, at least, isolate the months fairly accurately and give you an overall view of the year ahead. Clearly, some months will be fairly dull

or uneventful while others may indicate changes and developments.

You can also use the cards to indicate months of the year, or seasons, by working with the elemental connections. These methods are guidelines, described fully later on. You may want to develop your own techniques as you progress.

Preparing for a reading

Whether you are practising, or reading the cards for someone else, you should always prepare carefully. Take a few deep breaths, and sit quietly for a moment. If you are reading for someone else, ask the person to do the same before shuffling the cards. Both reader and inquirer should try to clear their minds, and relax before approaching the cards.

It is also very helpful to ask for some kind of guidance during these moments. You can mentally appeal to your higher self, deep mind, spirit guide, God, or whatever else appeals. You can request the cards to reveal information which will help you or the inquirer to resolve difficulties in the most positive way. You can also ask your own higher self to speak through the cards, and clarify matters requiring your attention.

When reading for someone else, you might like to ask for information which will help the person to progress on his or her path through life. These requests are rather like little prayers, easing you into a receptive intuitive frame of mind.

Other possible additional rituals include burning some incense, lighting a candle, or perhaps playing some uplifting orchestral music. Do what feels right for you, but make it a special moment or activity which divides consulting the Tarot from everyday concerns.

Always lay the cards on a clean, clear surface. Some people have special tablecloths on which the cards are laid, others always read the cards in a special place – which can even be on the floor. Make sure you have plenty of room, so that your cards are not crowded together – and you are physically comfortable while reading them.

Shuffling the Tarot

Shuffle the cards thoroughly, making sure some are reversed during this process. You can do this by what's known as 'washing the cards' – that is, placing them face down on a flat surface and moving them gently around in a clockwise direction, before gathering them up again into a pack. Otherwise, shuffle as normal but turn a few cards around during the process. If they want to come out, they will.

When reading for another person you can proceed in one of two ways. Some readers like to shuffle the cards themselves, and then present the deck to the querent for cutting. Others prefer the querent to shuffle the cards themselves. Neither way is right or wrong, so choose whichever method you find works for you. Reading the Tarot is a very personal activity, and ultimately you must base your decisions upon instinct and intuition.

The cards are cut with the left hand into three piles, and then put back together – making sure they are in a different order. If you, or your inquirer, is left-handed then use the right hand for this operation. This theoretically allows the intuitive side of our brains to 'choose' how the cards are arranged.

Choosing your significator

Some spreads require what is called a 'significator'. This card represents the inquirer in the reading, and can be chosen in various ways. To begin with, it is probably easiest to use the astrological correspondences. All you need to know is your inquirer's birth sign, and then you can choose the appropriate court card by referring to the descriptions on pages 124–135.

If this is not possible, then try to pick out basic personality traits and base your choice on this. You can also choose a court card to represent the general area of inquiry in a question.

For example, if the question relates to career matters the King or Queen of Wands might be the most suitable choice. Knights can be used to represent men in their teens and early twenties, while Queens represent women from their early twenties onwards. Young girls could be represented by one of the Pages.

Once chosen, do not simply place the significator on the table and forget all about him or her. Try to bring this card in as you make your interpretation by seeing how it relates to other cards in the layout.

Analysing your layout

CORRESPONDENCES WITH THE MINOR CARDS				
Suit	Wands	Swords	Pentacles	Cups
Element	Fire	Air	Earth	Water
Mode	Objective	Subjective	Objective	Subjective
Key	Action	Thought	Practicality	Emotion

Once the cards are laid out in front of you, look closely at them as a whole before starting to read them individually. First of all, check to see how many Major Arcana cards have appeared – if any. These cards highlight important events, shifts in attitude and outlook, and are concerned with much deeper levels than the Minor Arcana. If you have chosen a spread which has specific meanings attached to each position (such as the Horseshoe or Horoscope), a Major card will immediately show you where the emphasis of your reading lies.

If you are looking at a spread with inbuilt timing, such as the Romany, or Twelve Month or Calendar spreads, you can see quickly where the most challenging or meaningful moments occur by looking for the Major cards. Very often the Minor cards will serve to amplify one of the meanings attached to the complex Major cards.

So the next step is to look at the Minor cards, and see which ones have appeared next to your Major cards. They can show whether the Major card refers primarily to an inner or outer event.

A large number of Major cards indicates that the inquirer has reached a meaningful time in life. This may be difficult, or involve important changes such as marriage, children, or career upheaval. Such times are likely to be memorable, and great care must be taken when interpreting the cards for the inquirer is probably feeling particu-

larly uncertain about his or her future.

If there are a lot of Minor cards, you can concentrate more on everyday concerns. Events, thoughts and feelings indicated by these cards are, of course, important too. But they tend to be less influential in the long term, and are often concerned with now or the immediate future.

The Minor cards can also show you whether the reading is subjective or objective; whether it mainly concerns love, career, material goods or intellectual matters; and usually reveals which characters will play a crucial role in the inquirer's future. A glance at the chart will tell you which element gives further expression to the objective or subjective mode represented by the cards and how this manifests in life.

Minor Arcana
Resonance, dissonance, and majorities

When you first look at a spread of cards it is likely that one suit will predominate. This immediately gives you a rough idea of what the reading is about, and is called a Primary majority.

This suit is often accompanied by a noticeable number of cards from another suit, although there are less of them. This is called a Secondary majority.

These groups of cards can help you to see whether the reading mainly refers to subjective, inner thoughts (Swords) and feelings (Cups) – or is concentrating upon objective, tangible events (Wands and Pentacles). The Primary majority, therefore, will be either subjective or objective. The Secondary majority may be subjective too, indicating that the reading is concentrating on the way you (or the querent) think and feel about events. Or, it will be objective – indicating that outer events have an important bearing upon the spread.

For example, someone might be very unhappy, depressed and frustrated inside – although outwardly his or her life seems to contain all the right material ingredients for happiness. In this case, the person is involved with an inner struggle and must look closely at thoughts and feelings. Another person could be in need of sound practical advice about a change of job, move of home, or the health of someone close to them. Here you would be looking at the real world in an objective, practical way.

Obviously, a reading is often a mixture of both influences, especially when the cards have been consulted about general future issues. If a specific question was asked, then the minor cards should reveal which broad area of life this affects or refers to. So, a noticeable number of Pentacles would indicate practical concerns and money matters, while a noticeable number of Cups suggests relationships, creativity, and feelings are important to you or the querent.

The next step is to look for the Secondary majority. There are fewer of these cards, but they still form a noticeable group. They can indicate areas of secondary importance, or have a direct bearing upon the largest group.

Friends and enemies

Each suit is also strengthened, weakened, or remains neutral in the presence of other suits. This is known as resonance and dissonance, and basically transcends the individual meanings of the cards. It is rather like looking at a group of people. Some of these characters get on really well, and bring out the best in each other. Others find it more difficult to be friends, for they have less in common and find it hard to see one another's best points. Yet their individual talents and abilities remain fundamentally unchanged, they are simply positively or negatively affected by the company they keep.

Swords weaken Pentacles, for example, but strengthen Cups and Wands. So, if you saw the powerful Ace of Swords surrounded by solid, realistic Pentacles, its overall influence and strength would be weakened – and less emphasis placed upon it as part of your interpretation. But if you saw it surrounded by Wands or Cups these would serve to highlight its meaning and effect upon the whole spread.

Understanding these principles may seem complicated at first. But it can improve the accuracy of your interpretation, and help you make sense of the overall feeling of any particular spread. The following chart sets out key phrases which describe all the basic pairs of suits you will encounter in your readings. These provide you with a category, while the individual cards and combinations spell out the details of the story before you.

How to use the chart

To use the chart below, look up your Primary majority along the top. Then find your Secondary majority in the column at the side, run your eye (or finger) along until you find the section beneath your primary column. The information there will tell you whether the two suits are compatible and

strengthen one another – resonant; whether they are neutral; or whether they detract from one another – dissonant. It will also give you a very general key phrase describing the type of spread before you.

This description may be be likened to a season of the year. Everyone has a pretty good idea what winter is like in the northern hemisphere – the days are shorter, the temperature drops, most plants are dormant and so on. Yet some winters are hard and bitter, with heavy snow and freezing temperatures. Others are mild and rainy.

So it is with the cards. A spread full of Cups and Pentacles is concentrating on emotion, creativity, and practical, financial matters. There, in effect, is your 'season'. But for a more exact description you must look at which specific cards have appeared, how they combine with each other, and whether they are upright or reversed. This is your 'weather report'.

RELATIONSHIPS BETWEEN THE SUITS OF THE MINOR ARCANA				
SUIT	**WANDS**	**SWORDS**	**PENTACLES**	**CUPS**
WANDS	Neutral	Strengthened	Strengthened	Weakened
Key	Energy/Career/Deals	Visions and Ideas	Cash and Career	Unstable Emotions
SWORDS	Strengthened	Neutral	Weakened	Strengthened
Key	Ideas and Energy	Discord/Decisions/ Mental Activity	Material versus Mental	Creativity/Ideas
PENTACLES	Strengthened	Weakened	Neutral	Neutral
Key	Practical Energy	Thinking versus Reality	Money/Property/Practicality	Feelings/Family/Finance
CUPS	Weakened	Strengthened	Neutral	Neutral
Key	Unstable Emotions/ Creativity	Blends logic with emotion	Realistic Emotions/ Creativity	Highlights Emotion/ Creativity

Where a spread is mainly composed of only one suit, the overall meaning of your spread is dictated by that suit. This happens in spreads where there are perhaps only one or two cards representing other suits.

A quick guide to basic Tarot reading

1 Choose the right deck for you, and enjoy getting to know it.

2 Develop your intuition, alongside learning the meanings of the cards. The more practice you get, the better you will become.

3 Prepare carefully for your readings, and create your own little rituals. These will help to make Tarot reading a special

activity, and set it apart from your everyday routine.

4 Choose your Tarot layout, and any significator, to suit the circumstances. Generally, it is best to begin with an overall view, and then proceed to isolate particularly important matters.

5 Have a good look at the whole spread first. A lot of Major Arcana cards indicate that a significant time lies ahead. Mostly Minor cards suggest that the reading is more concerned with events which will prove to be unimportant in the long term.

Check to see which elements are represented by the Minor cards. What do these represent? Is there a Primary Majority, and if so, what is it? The proceed to the Secondary Majority, if any, and ask the same question. Are they compatible, or do they exert a weakening effect on each other?

6 Now you are ready to begin reading individual cards. Remember to interpret them in the right context. Consider the meaning of the position they occupy, especially in layouts like the Celtic Cross. Then see how they work with adjoining cards, and how they relate to the significator – if there is one.

7 During the reading let your logical, critical everyday mind take a back seat. Relax, and allow your intuition to make connections between the images and symbols before you. Try not to allow your conscious knowledge of the situation or your inquirer to influence you. Everyone's life contains a few surprises; often the most unlikely prediction or interpretation turns out to be the right one. Have fun.

Above: Aleister Crowley's Thoth deck, c. 1943

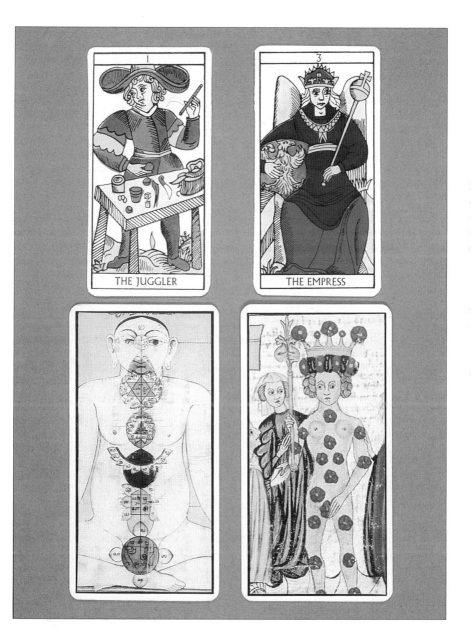

Above: The Esoteric deck compared with the traditional Marseilles cards, The Juggler and The Empress

THE SIX MONTH SPECIAL

TWO GENERAL–PURPOSE SPREADS

ABOUT THE SPREAD

This spread employs 21 cards, laid out in seven vertical columns comprising three cards per column (see diagram).

Column one: *The self*
This column tells you what is on someone's mind at the present time, and what areas of life the person is particularly concerned with. It often indicates new mental and emotional developments which the querent may be barely conscious of. Such developments would include blossoming creativity, intuition, ambition or even negative thoughts and feelings.

Column two: *What's closest to you*
This column deals with personal relationships, close friendships, and sometimes important colleagues. The context should be clear from the surrounding cards. If these three cards seem very impersonal, then relationships may be temporarily unimportant or peacefully settled and stable. In this case, the column refers to the general environment – home, work, or social life.

Column three: *Hopes and fears*
        or dreams and wishes
The title of this column is self-explanatory. It is often very revealing, however, especially when read in combination with column one.

Column four: *What you expect*
This column reveals the progress of known plans, activities and events. These are things which are expected to happen, although they may not of course. This is the column for news of success, conclusions of plans already in motion, and also for delays and changes.

Column five: *What you do not expect*
Here is the column which reveals destiny or karma in action. It often contains surprises, relates to totally unexpected events, or further elaborates on changes indicated in column four.

Column six: *Near future*
Events or developments which can be expected over the next two or three months are indicated here. Sometimes this column reveals things which are imminent, and may even occur the following day or week.

Column seven: *Further future*
This column usually refers to events four to six months in the future. Look carefully at columns four, five, and six to see whether there is any connection and if so, where. Sometimes little connection will be apparent, do not worry – simply choose another spread which will amplify matters once you have finished reading this one.

Below and opposite: *A six-month special spread.*
1 four of Cups; *2* eight of Cups; *3* four of Wands; *4* eight of Wands; *5* nine of Wands; *6* ten of wands; *7* Knight of Wands; *8* Page of Wands; *9* three of Swords; *10* two of Pentacles; *11* the Empress; *12* the Lovers; *13* Justice; *14* seven of Wands; *15* five of Wands; *16* Knight of Swords; *17* five of Cups; *18* Death; *19* the Moon; *20* Knight of Cups; *21* three of Wands.

1	4	7	10	13	16	19
2	5	8	11	14	17	20
3	6	9	12	15	18	21

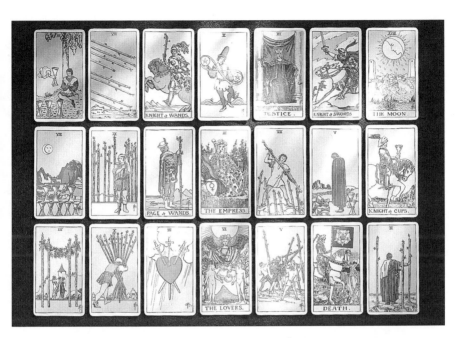

PAST, PRESENT AND FUTURE
– a Romany spread

Here the 21 cards are laid out in three horizontal lines (see diagram) indicating past, present and future. Again, the future cards tend to relate to the near future – up to about six months. This spread can be a useful one to start a session, for it provides a good basic framework – and reveals what influence past problems or situations are having upon present and future events.

Always look to see where the card which most appropriately represents yourself or your querent falls. Is it in the past, present or future? This will give you an idea of whether someone is attached to his or her memories, is firmly living in the present, or is constantly hoping and dreaming about tomorrow. Sometimes, there may be no such significator. This can indicate detachment or a balanced view of life. If you are reading for an older person, it can denote a greater interest in the lives of children and grandchildren. Such people feel they have lived their own lives, and are now taking a back seat.

1	2	3	4	5	6	7
8	9	10	11	12	13	14
15	16	17	18	19	20	21

Top and above: In the basic Romany spread, the 21 cards are laid out in three horizontal lines, indicating past, present and future. The future cards tend to relate to the near future. Always check where the card which represents yourself or your querent falls.

THE HOROSCOPE
LOOKING WITHIN

ABOUT THE SPREAD

The Horoscope or Zodiac spread is an excellent one to begin with. Each card is placed in a position which corresponds to one of the twelve houses of the horoscope. Each house, and therefore each card position, relates to a designated area of life – so the card which falls there should be read in this context. As you become more familiar with the cards you can add to this circle by placing a second and third card in each position to amplify the information.

This spread requires a deliberately-chosen significator, which is placed in the centre of your circle. Since it is inspired by astrology, it would be most appropriate to choose this representative by sign and element from the Court cards. These correspondences are given on page 72-80.

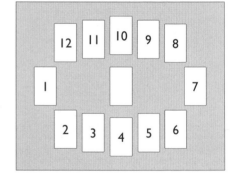

Top and above: 1 seven of Wands; **2** Queen of Swords; **3** the Magician; **4** the Hierophant; **5** two of Pentacles; **6** three of Swords; **7** the Sun reversed; **8** the High Priestess; **9** the Lovers reversed; **10** five of Cups; **11** Knight of Swords; **12** five of Wands.

Position 1: *The First House*
Ruling sign: ARIES The self
This position describes your inquirer, how the person is currently thinking and feeling, and often reveals how he or she is approaching the challenges and problems. It should be read in conjunction with the chosen significator to see how this card amplifies or contradicts the qualities shown there.

For example, if your chosen card is the Queen of Pentacles – denoting a practical, earthy woman – and the card in position 1 is the eight of Wands you would be looking at someone whose down-to-earth approach is lightened by a great energy, and a marked ability to communicate. If, however, the card in position 1 is the two of Swords – which does not combine happily with the suit of pentacles – your querent's basic need for security could be undermined by mental stress, or tension caused by worry over another person.

Position 2: *The Second House*
Ruling sign: TAURUS Resources and money
This position denotes finances, material goods and our attitudes towards these things. Whatever falls here will either refer to your inquirer's financial situation, or reveal his or her feelings towards earnings and belongings at the present time.

Generally, Wands or Pentacles indicate that you are looking at real, practical matters here – while Swords or Cups will reflect inner beliefs and concerns. Major cards clearly point to an area of great significance, and may suggest deeper psychological interpretations. Such interpretations might stress attitudes towards innate talents, spiritual wealth or poverty, and reveal how well someone copes with physical reality.

Position 3: *The Third House*
Ruling sign: GEMINI Communications
This position relates to communications such as letters, telephone calls and visits. It is also concerned with short journeys, weekends away, and travelling connected with work. Movement and energy are connected with this position, particularly mental energy and the flow of ideas and information in someone's life.

Cards here may simply indicate news about outer events, people or projects coming into focus. They can also suggest how someone communicates, and whether this is especially important in relation to character or job.

Position 4: *The Fourth House*
Ruling sign: CANCER Home
This position refers to the home, thoughts and feelings about it, about parents, and any brothers and sisters. The emotions are strongly stressed here, for this position denotes much more than just bricks and mortar. It describes someone's life at home, and feelings about its quality.

Moves, financial matters and property deals are more usually found in position 2. This placement can also reveal childhood associations with the emotive concept of 'home' as a safe place or refuge, as well as describing current home life.

Position 5: *The Fifth House*
Ruling sign: LEO Pleasure, romance and creativity
This position denotes love, pleasure, romance, and creativity. Since many of the cards which relate to love, such as the Ace of Cups, are also linked with creativity you must read this card very carefully or you could end up mistakenly predicting a romantic love-affair for a happily-married artist who is about to embark upon his or her great work.

To decide exactly which area the card refers to, look carefully at position 10 – career – and position 7, partnerships. Which area seems to be more important? Are there any Resonant or Dissonant cards? Are there any Major cards? Were there any problems regarding love or career in position 1? Let your knowledge of the cards and your intuition guide you, and the connections should fall into place.

Position 6: *The Sixth House*
Ruling sign: VIRGO Health and work
This position relates to health matters and day-to-day work. Health should be read on every level and not confined to physical interpretations. Look and see whether the card denotes the mental, emotional, or physical realms. It may even refer to spiritual or psychic health, too. Pentacles in this position usually indicate earning a living,

work, and sometimes training or studying.

It is important to remember that these are immediate concerns and do not describe the inquirer's career in its broadest sense. Many famous composers and authors had fairly dull jobs, for instance, which enabled them to support themselves while pursuing their true 'career'.

Position 7: *The Seventh House*
Ruling sign: LIBRA Partnerships
This is the position of joint ventures, husbands and wives, marriage and all formal partnerships. Cards here often represent the actual partner, or feelings and attitudes towards that person. It should be fairly simple to decide whether the position is referring to an emotional partnership, or a business-orientated one. Positions 1, 4, and 10 should help you decide.

You should also look again at position 5 – does it indicate emotional pleasures or blocks and difficulties? If it looks good, while position 7 indicates trouble, it is unlikely to connect with the querent's marriage or permanent partnership. In this case, it will refer to work or creative links.

Position 8: The Eight House
Ruling sign: SCORPIO Sex, death and money
This is the position of deaths, major changes, inheritance and sexuality. It covers three of the most taboo subjects in our society – death, sex and money – so go carefully when you are interpreting it. Also be certain to check, if a Minor card falls here, whether you are dealing with a subjective (Sword and Cups) or objective (Wands and Pentacles) interpretation. A real inheritance, for example, is more than likely to be represented here by the ten of Pentacles. But false hopes of an inheritance might be suggested by the seven of Cups, denoting fairy gold.

Position 9: *The Ninth House*
Ruling sign: SAGITTARIUS The far horizons
This position refers to long distance travel, philosophy of life, education and future hopes. Again, you should look carefully at the card before deciding which category it falls into. Real, physical travel is usually very simple to read – but often entails changes in circumstance and mental out-

look too. So remember that the ninth position also deals with mental and spiritual travelling before committing yourself to describing a simple trip on an aeroplane.

Position 10: *The Tenth House*
Ruling sign: CAPRICORN Career
This position relates to career in the broadest sense, and reveals how someone approaches this area of life. Ambition, the ability to work hard towards a goal, and the type of organizations and talents involved can all be represented here. Cards here may also suggest how important a career is to your querent. Imagination is needed to interpret this position, for some people may not have a career in the conventional sense of the word. Do not fall into the modern trap of equating career with earning a living.

Housewives and mothers, retired people, and students fall into this awkward category. In these cases, you are primarily looking at how they operate in the wider world around them; what interests them; and what concerns them – developing creativity, caring for the environment, charities and political movements may all be represented.

Position 11: *The Eleventh House*
Ruling sign: AQUARIUS Friends
This position refers to friends, and all groups gathered together for social or ideological purposes. It can represent communities; colleagues; fellow students; or simply suggest the kind of social life someone enjoys – or is currently experiencing.

Position 12: *The Twelfth House*
Ruling sign: PISCES What is hidden
This can be a revealing position, referring as it does to one's hidden fears, unconscious wishes, and also to limitations and blocks. This is the position of what is hidden, hard to talk about, secret or repressed. Therefore, great sensitivity is required when reading the card which falls here – especially if it belongs to the Major Arcana. You should also see how the meaning of this card connects with your significator, and also how it colours the rest of the spread.

ANSWERING QUESTIONS
THE CELTIC CROSS

ABOUT THE SPREAD

The Celtic Cross is probably one of the best-known ways of laying out the Tarot cards, and is said to be ancient. A. E. Waite, who directed the designs of the Tarot deck named after him at the beginning of the century expressed strong approval of the spread. It is certainly a good, reliable method to use when you want to answer a specific question.

HOW TO ASK YOUR QUESTION

To begin with, the querent should clearly frame a question, so that it is unambiguous. You will not receive a clear answer if your enquiry contains lots of ifs and buts. For instance, supposing you had to choose between two jobs, which on the surface appeared to be pretty similar. In this kind of situation, you should separate the two choices, asking one question for each job rather than one compound question: 'Should I take job A or job B?' Similar rules apply to the Chinese oracle, the I Ching, and to the Celtic runes.

Choose your significator from amongst the court cards. You can either use the astrological correspondences for this, or select the significator by carefully considering your inquirer's attitudes towards this question, and the relevant area of life. For example, a question concerning money would be best represented by one of the suit of Pentacles. Lay this card face up on the table in front of you, and you are ready to begin.

TRADITIONAL MEANINGS

Shuffle and cut the cards, concentrating upon the question as you do so. When you are ready, take the first card from the top of the deck and place it face up across the significator. Traditionally, at this point the reader says 'This covers him'. If you have a strong sense of drama, and enjoy the ritual

aspects of card reading you may like to learn the phrases for placing each of the ten cards. More retiring souls may baulk at this theatrical approach; rest assured that it is not strictly necessary. For those who wish to use them, the traditional phrases are given in the following description.

LAYING OUT THE CELTIC CROSS

After selecting the significator from the court cards, the shuffled and cut cards are placed in the sequence and positions shown in the diagram on page 157, using the phrases below.

Card 1: This covers him/her
Card 2: This crosses him/her
Card 3: This crowns him/her
Card 4: This is beneath him/her
Card 5: This is behind him/her
Card 6: This is before him/her
Card 7: Yourself
Card 8: The House
Card 9: Hopes and Fears
Card 10: What will come

INTERPRETING THE POSITIONS

Card 1: This card often reveals the substance of the question, and indicates the kind of atmosphere surrounding it. It is a card firmly rooted in the present and may denote the inquirer's state of mind, outside influences upon the question, and whether there are positive or negative forces at work at the moment.

Card 2: This card denotes obstacles, blocks and potential opposition surrounding the inquirer. Sometimes, of course, this card will be positive and thus harder to read as an obstacle. A favourable 'cross' indicates that there is little opposition. However, do not get carried away – remember that even a vibrant card like the Sun contains warnings against excess.

You should also look to see how this card relates to both significator and Card 1. Do they belong to harmonious minor suits? What is their combined message? If your significator was the Queen of Cups, for instance, the positive presence of the Ace of Wands might be undermined a little and its interpretation should be modified accordingly.

Card 3: This card relates to conscious plans and intentions, and often indicates developments in the near future – although not the final outcome to the question.

Card 4: This card describes what kind of past influences have led to the present situation, or have a significant bearing upon it. It can represent the inquirer's state of mind, or actual events and activities which are still affecting matters today. Sometimes the inquirer is unaware of these things, and may be surprised or puzzled by this card.

Card 5: Factors which are now passing away are shown by this card. Sometimes they are clearly in the past, at other times the inquirer may still believe they are influencing his or her situation. However, this position denotes the past, and is particularly reassuring if the card here is negative.

Card 6: Fresh influences, new people, and future events are denoted by this card. It is helpful to read it in combination with Card 3, so that you can see whether the inquirer's plans are going to be helped or hindered by forthcoming circumstances.

Card 7: This card reveals the inquirer's present state of mind, position, or feelings about the matter in hand. It should be read with specific reference to the significator, and Cards 1, 2, 3 and 4. This should give you a good picture of the general conditions surrounding the question as the inquirer sees it. Remember that a good deal depends upon mental attitude, clarity of purpose, self-confidence and awareness. Someone who is in a negative or depressed frame of mind may find it difficult to make the most of the best opportunities.

Card 8: This card represents the inquirer's surroundings, and often suggests what the attitudes and actions of other people will be in relation to the question. Any helpful, or unhelpful influences around the inquirer should be revealed here. It can also show how others see the inquirer – which can be very different from how the inquirer sees himself or herself.

Card 9: This card indicates the inquirer's hopes,

fears and expectations regarding the question. Have a look at Card 3 to see how closely these deeper feelings relate to more obvious, planned intentions.

Someone could be asking about moving house, for instance. On the surface, the intention to move could appear to be serious – estate agents have been contacted, properties viewed, and the person's present home has been put on the market. But underneath he or she may not want to move at all. Perhaps a strong emotional attachment to the old home or neighbourhood prevails. Perhaps the person is just afraid of uprooting from a familiar environment. These fears need to be confronted, for they affect the outcome and also create stress.

Card 10: This card should give you the most likely future result, the outcome of the question, and reveal whether it will benefit the inquirer or not. If you get a court card here, or even a Major Arcana card which seems to indicate a person rather than a situation, you will need to do another spread.

But before doing this, do remember that all the court cards have abstract meanings. Should these meanings seem inappropriate, take the tenth card and use it as the significator in your next layout. This second layout should reveal what effect this person will have on the inquirer's question. It will relate entirely to this individual, revealing his or her attitudes and actions as they affect the matter in hand.

Right: The Celtic Cross, or Grand Cross, was recommended for answering questions by Arthur Edward Waite, who was part of the short-lived but influential magic order of the Golden Dawn, founded at the end of the nineteenth century. Later, Waite devised the Tarot deck named after him, which was designed under his direction by Pamela Colman Smith.

Above and below: The diagram identifies the cards in the photograph of the Celtic Cross spread.
1 the Fool; 2 ten of Cups; 3 six of Wands;
4 Page of Swords; 5 the Lovers reversed; 6 nine of Pentacles; 7 five of Pentacles; 8 Justice; 9 six of Cups;
10 Queen of Cups.

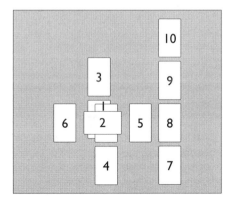

THE HORSESHOE

ASK A QUESTION

ABOUT THE SPREAD

This is a very simple spread which is useful for answering questions. It is particularly suitable for beginners, since it does not contain too many cards. You can look up each card in turn, and relate its meaning to the position quickly. And since each position represents a distinct sphere of influence, you can easily discard meanings which seem inappropriate.

ASKING YOUR QUESTION

As in the case of the Celtic Cross spread on pages 155–7, the question needs to be unambiguously framed. Remember, the clarity of the answer depends on the clarity of the question: if two choices are involved ask one question for each of them.

Here are three versions of the Horseshoe; one general, classic one; one for career questions and one designed with relationship questions in mind.

THE CLASSIC HORSESHOE

Card 1: The past
Card 2: The present
Card 3: Hidden influences
Card 4: Obstacles
Card 5: The environment, and attitudes of other people
Card 6: What should be done
Card 7: The most likely result

THE LOVE HORSESHOE

Card 1: The past – this shows the foundations of the relationship.

Card 2: The present – how the inquirer sees his or her relationship now. Remember that this card is usually very subjective since it refers to someone's view of his or her partner, which may not represent reality.

Card 3: Hopes, fears and expectations – this shows what kind of dreams and beliefs the inquirer is bringing to the relationship, and may reveal unconscious patterns of behaviour.

Card 4: Areas of conflict – this can be entirely mental or emotional, or suggest financial or other practical problems, such as clashing careers, religious differences and so on.

Card 5: Outside influences – what worldly factors are affecting the relationship. These can range from a former marriage, to the effect any children, in-laws, or even friends and colleagues may be having on the relationship.

Card 6: The best current course of action.

Card 7: Probable outcome if this course of action is taken.

THE WORK HORSESHOE

Card 1: Past influences upon your problem or dilemma.

Card 2: The present situation.

Card 3: What is most positive about this situation. This may include talents and abilities, a sense of security, or represent some kind of challenge which the inquirer needs in order to progress.

Card 4: What is most difficult about this situation. This represents inner problems such as low self-confidence, boredom, inability to settle, being in the wrong job area and so on. If a very positive card appears here then there is little opposition and few blocks to long-term progress. The problem may then be due to factors outside the querent's control, for which see Card 5.

Card 5: Outside factors. These can range from the current economic situation to jealousy at work. Positive outside factors include unexpected help, job offers, and opportunities for further training.

Card 6: Best course of action at present.

Card 7: Probable result.

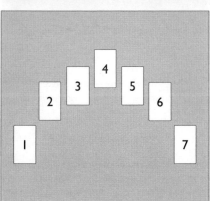

The diagram shows you how to lay out the cards and identifies those in the Horseshoe spread shown in the photograph. **1** the Emperor reversed; **2** two of Swords; **3** Temperance; **4** three of Wands; **5** Knight of Cups; **6** the Moon; **7** Death.

THE CALENDAR
TIMING AND TAROT LAYOUTS

ABOUT THE SPREAD

The Calendar layout looks exactly like the Horoscope spread; there are 12 cards in a circle with one in the middle. But this time each card represents a month of the year, beginning with whichever month you are currently in. If you like, you can choose a significator as before and place it in the centre of the circle before you begin.

However, I have found that it is more interesting to let the Tarot speak freely here, and simply lay the thirteenth card in the centre. This card then represents the overall feeling or theme of the year ahead, and often indicates which area of life will be uppermost in the inquirer's mind and pattern of fate.

You can also carry on dealing round the circle a second and third time, so that there are three cards for each month – and three cards in the centre. This should expand the original information somewhat – although it is too complicated for absolute beginners.

WHEN TO USE THE CALENDAR

This layout is a good one to use after you have done a general spread such as the Tree of Life, or the Horoscope. It is effective if you have noticed a significant future event in the Romany spread, but are unable to pinpoint the exact timing.

The Calendar can also be used when someone wants to find out when he or she will move home, or job. It is also quite helpful when you want to discern the probable future pattern of a difficult relationship. And if a new and important lover is on the horizon, this spread should indicate when romance will finally blossom.

TIMING AND THE MINOR ARCANA

Since each suit of the Minor Arcana corresponds to an element, which in turn is linked with a

season of the year, it is possible to use it to answer the question 'when?'. The first method uses the twos, threes and fours of each suit, and is very simple and basic. The correspondences are as follows:

The suit of Pentacles: *Winter*
TWO: December
THREE: January
FOUR: February

The suit of Swords: *Spring*
TWO: March
THREE: April
FOUR: May

The suit of Wands: *Summer*
TWO: June
THREE: July
FOUR: August

The suit of Cups: *Autumn*
TWO: September
THREE: October
FOUR: November

METHOD

Shuffle the whole deck, concentrating upon the question. Cut the cards into three, using the left hand (unless left–handed, in which case the right hand should be used) and reassemble the deck in a different order.

Now start turning up the cards from the top until you have counted off 13 cards, stopping if a card of the month has appeared – in which case you have your answer. Should no such card appear, start a fresh pile of 13. If this pile is empty too, commence a third. Should this pile fail to reveal the answer, the matter is still undecided or unlikely to happen within the next 12–month period.

THE FOUR ACES

A similar method employs the four aces, each of which represents a season of the year. This method is slightly more sophisticated in that it can

can also answer 'yes' or 'no', as well as 'when'. Separate the deck, discarding the Major Arcana. Shuffle well, making sure some cards are reversed as you do so. Cut as usual, and begin dealing the cards into a pile of 13 until you reach an ace. If it is upright, the answer to your question is 'yes', if reversed, 'no'.

Should no aces appear in the first pile, continue with a second and third pile of 13. Again, if no aces appear a definite answer to your question is not possible at the moment. You will probably need to do another type of spread to find out why this is so. If you received a definite 'no', it is also advisable to investigate further to discover potential problems, blocks, or other avenues which could be explored. If you received a 'yes', and would like to known when your wish will be granted, look at the ace you have drawn, and refer to its seasonal correspondence. These are: Ace of Pentacles, winter; Ace of Swords, spring; Ace of Wands, summer; and Ace of Cups, autumn.

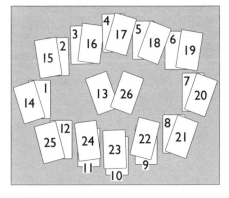

The numbered key above shows you how to lay out the cards to form the Calendar spread in the photograph - in which each card represents a month of the year - expanded by dealing round the circle a second time to give two cards per month.

THE TREE OF LIFE
WHERE YOU STAND NOW

ABOUT THE SPREAD

This spread is based on the pattern of the cabalistic Tree of Life, and contains ten cards – each relating to a sphere of life (see diagram). This is a simplified version of the layout, designed to give you an overall view of someone's current situation and concerns. Like the Horoscope layout, it is a good one to choose to begin a reading.

INTERPRETING THE POSITIONS

Card 1 represents the inquirer's spiritual world; his or her attitudes towards it, and general inner state of being at the time of the reading.

Card 2 denotes energy, drive, and spheres of responsibility.

Card 3 relates to understanding, and represents limiting or containing factors operating in the inquirer's life.

Card 4 represents financial matters, and practical activities.

Card 5 denotes strife, challenges and indicates what kind of opposition must be overcome by the inquirer.

Card 6 refers to the inquirer's achievements, successes, and outer image.

Card 7 represents the inquirer's love life, emotional attachments and feelings about this side of life in general.

Card 8 denotes worldly matters concerning the inquirer; business and career; cultural or artistic endeavour – and indicates how these are being approached.

Card 9 represents the unconscious mind and all its secrets and hidden depths. It can also refer to health matters, especially when these concern overall well-being.

Card 10 indicates the inquirer's roots, and denotes home, family, and close relationships.

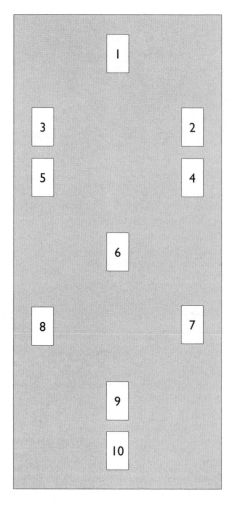

The diagram illustrates the order of laying out the cards for the Tree of Life spread.

SAMPLE SPREADS
THE TAROT IN LOVE

A QUESTION OF LOVE

Here is an example of how the Love Horseshoe works in answer to a specific question about a relationship. The inquirer was a woman in her late twenties who, although reasonably settled with her partner, had some gnawing doubts about the future of her relationship. Her question was, 'Where is my relationship going?'.

Card 1: *The Devil*
This shows that, in the past, the relationship had a passionately physical basis and that it tended to be obsessive – certainly on the part of the inquirer. She was initially infatuated with her boyfriend, and failed to see him as he really was. However, the attraction was so powerful that there was little she could do to avoid getting deeply involved.

Card 2: *Justice*
This card clearly demonstrates her need to make a decision, to find some kind of balance in the situation, and suggests that she would like to marry her boyfriend rather than simply live with him. But she still seems to be living in a dream-world where the relationship is concerned, for Justice is quite a cold, detached card. She has decided that their association has continued long enough for marriage to be the likely outcome; she would prefer to be married and would like her boyfriend to agree.

Card 3: *The six of Swords*
Here is further confirmation of her rather unrealistic attitudes towards the relationship. She hopes that marriage will provide her with an escape route, a passage away from difficulties.

Card 4: *The Queen of Wands*
The presence of the Queen of Wands suggests

that another woman – or the memory of one – is coming between this couple. Indeed, it turned out that the boyfriend had been married before and that our inquirer felt insecure about this. However, it also explained the boyfriend's hesitation, and fear of making a second mistake.

Card 5: *The Hanged Man*
This shows the attitudes of other people to our inquirer's dilemma. Clearly, others believe that she has reached a plateau, that there is little possibility of her circumstances changing, and that progress is suspended for the time being. Some people may believe that she is sacrificing any possibility of getting married by staying with this man. These views are influencing her, and confirming her own worst fears.

Card 6: *The Hermit*
The Hermit highlights the best course of action open to this woman, which is to calm down, be quiet, and listen to her own inner voice. Someone is likely to offer wise advice very soon, and she should pay attention to it if she wishes to resolve matters. It might be a good idea to go away for a few days, too, in order to give both partners some breathing space.

Card 7: *The three of Cups*
Here is the result, and final answer to her question. This card suggests a happy outcome, after a period of withdrawal suggested by the Hermit. There is a celebration, and an engagement is extremely likely.

THE HOROSCOPE SPREAD
an example

Here the querant was a man in his mid-thirties, a Sagittarian by birth. The King of Wands was chosen as the significator, and placed in the centre of the circle.

Position 1: The seven of Wands appears in the first position, indicating that this fiery man is facing some challenges in his life. He is certainly fighting for his own ideas, and although things are not easy for him he is likely to succeed in the end.

Position 2: The Queen of Swords suggests that he has a good relationship with money, although it is not particularly important to him. Swords and Wands are compatible suits, but Swords belong to the mental realms.

Therefore, this position should be read in terms of intellectual wealth and resources rather than bank balance. Here, this card suggests excellent communication skills, and success connected with writing, academic matters, or public speaking.

Position 3: The presence of the Magician in this position confirms the meaning of position 2. He further indicates that this man has a quick and clever mind, would make a good agent or entrepreneur, and is adept at organizing things to suit himself. So, despite the challenges and changes indicated by the first card, this man seems to have his career under control in the long term.

Position 4: The Hierophant in position 4 suggest that this man is rather conventional at home. Status and position are important to him; his home and marriage reflect these beliefs. He also needs the outer stability a comfortable home represents, he enjoys routine here in contrast to his rather unstable, fiery career.

Position 5: The two of Pentacles resonates with the Magician, for in some ways it is the Minor Arcana's equivalent. Appearing in the position which denotes pleasure, it suggests a fondness for gambling.

Position 6: The three of Hearts appears in the position connected with our inquirer's work and health. It suggests some degree of mental conflict, already hinted at by the seven of Wands in position 1. Quarrels at work are likely, and the inquirer may be leaving his job soon since this card can mean a separation. Changes are in the air.

Position 7: The Sun, reversed, appears here suggesting that – despite some passing strife and conflict all is basically well with partnership matters. Certainly, a solid marriage is suggested by the Hierophant, and this card serves to confirm that. In addition, problems with a business partnership would seem to be temporary, and should resolve themselves eventually.

Position 8: The High Priestess falls in the eighth place, suggesting a secretive attitude towards matters governed by this position. There is even the possibility of a fantasy woman or secret lover in this man's life.

Position 9: Here, the presence of the Lovers reversed confirms the possibilities of an illicit relationship. This position, dealing as it does with dreams and ideals, suggests that the affair is very idealistic – if misguided, and possibly dangerous. As we have already seen, a stable home is very important to this man. Yet his marriage and family have failed to satisfy his deeper ideals, and he is seeking these through this affair. Since both cards belong to the Major Arcana, this is not a lighthearted association – but serious and meaningful.

Position 10: The Five of Cups reveals how disillusioned our inquirer is with his career. He feels his hopes have little chance of success, and is rather depressed and forlorn about his direction in life. However, there is a light at the end of the tunnel; his partnership is basically sound, his talents are well-developed, and there is no indication of financial hardship.

Position 11: Here the Knight of Swords reveals a busy, active social life. The inquirer is surrounded by people, and there should be plenty of invitations and contacts to lift his depression over career matters.

Position 12: The Five of Wands falls in the position that denotes secrets, hidden fears and limitations. It echoes the persistent theme of conflict running through this spread, for it is an unstable fiery card denoting change and strife. This card confirms the challenges facing the inquirer, and suggests that he is battling with the discovery of new desires and ambitions.

He is not comfortable with these impulses, and may be feeling confused and uncertain. Although he is seeking something outside himself through a compelling and important love affair, and is trying to control his career, there are few certainties in his life at present. There is also the considerable conflict between his need for a stable home life, revealed by the Hierophant, and his pressing fantasies and love of mystery, symbolized by the High Priestess.

TAKING A CLOSER LOOK

This initial reading shows that further layouts are necessary. There are various ways of approaching the next stage; here are two simple methods which would be suitable.

First of all, we shall look more closely at his career problems. Having already established that he is talented, but disillusioned, the next step is to see whether he is on the right path – or whether he should make some sweeping changes. His question was 'Should I set up my own business?'

The Celtic Cross was chosen as the most suitable spread, and the King of Wands retained as the significator. This was his answer:

1 *This covers him:* the Fool, reversed, appeared in the first position, indicating that the inquirer could be presently wasting his abilities, and scattering his energies. He is restless, and needs a number of different projects to satisfy his wideranging mind. Making a big change would not be a good idea in the short term, however, since the Fool reversed warns against impetuous behaviour. He must wait for a little while longer.

2 *This crosses him:* the ten of Cups, the 'wish card', is hardly an obstacle at first glance. But since it falls in this position, it suggests that the inquirer's dreams and ambitions may be preventing him from getting on with his working life. In addition, Cups combined with Wands signify a changeable, emotional atmosphere surrounding our inquirer which is further confirmed by the presence of the Fool. The inquirer needs to become more realistic and down-to-earth if his plans are to come to anything. The most encouraging news is that there are few obstacles to success in the long term.

3 *This crowns him:* the six of Wands augurs cheering news, and further suggests that the inquirer should soon be able to put some of his plans into action. They will be successful, and his idea of starting a business would seem to be in tune with the times. As long as he bears the various warnings in mind, all should be well.

4 *This is beneath him:* the Page of Swords denotes that the inquirer has been thinking about this change for some time. He has changed his mind about his present work, probably because he no longer finds it mentally challenging.

5 *This is behind him:* the Lovers reversed appears for the second time, but in a different context. It reveals that – on a subconscious level – he has made up his mind. The disruptive battle with himself may still be going on, but somewhere deep inside he has reached a decision, and it is now a matter of implementing it at the right time.

6 *This is before him:* the nine of Pentacles brings a reassuringly worldly note into the spread. There is money on the horizon – he could even be made redundant from his job and be able to use some of the redundancy payment as capital. Here is the most likely interpretation of the good news augured by the six of Wands. This is particularly reassuring for him, because he has drawn the unhappy, poverty-stricken five of Pentacles in seventh place.

7 *The self:* the five of Pentacles suggests that he has a deep-rooted fear of poverty, and that this could be holding him back. As we saw in his Horoscope spread, a stable, conventional home and material well-being is important to him.

This card also indicates that his needs in this department are based to a certain extent on fear. Perhaps he knew poverty as a child; whatever the reason his fears are unreasonable and represent a limiting factor in his cards.

8 *The environment:* Justice denotes that other people see the inquirer as fair-minded and balanced. There could also be some useful contact with lawyers, or favourable legal settlements of some kind. The potential of unearned money indicated by the nine of Pentacles is enhanced by Justice; there should be a financially-rewarding decision in his favour soon.

9 *Hopes and fears:* the six of Cups shows that the inquirer is hoping to use old contacts and associations to help him in his future business. He feels that he has laid some useful foundations in the past, and may now expect to call in a few favours he thinks are owing.

10 *The result:* the Queen of Cups, read as an abstract card, denotes imagination and fantasy will be important ingredients of this business. It could even have innovative, 'New Age' overtones. She also suggests that this venture will bring the inquirer emotional satisfaction – something he does not receive from his work at the moment.

In conclusion, the answer is positive. He should start his own business, but would be wise to hang on to his old job for a while longer since it seems very likely that he will be made redundant

EMOTIONAL PROBLEMS

This man's emotional problems are extremely complex. Although they are causing him considerable conflict, he does not seem ready to make a decision at this point.

In this case the cards cannot be used to predict the final outcome for there are too many people involved. Some buried personal myth or pattern seems to be surfacing, and needs to be worked out. When consulting the Tarot about this kind of situation it is important not to be judgmental, or allow your own moral views to intrude.

The best approach here is to simply find out what he should do for the time being. He may

decide to seek professional counselling; this is probably his best option in the long term – but he must choose to do this for himself, when he feels ready for it.

A classic Horseshoe pattern was chosen. Here is what the cards revealed:

1: The Past is represented by the Emperor, reversed. This suggests a number of things; the inquirer may have entered his marriage while still rather immature – which is fairly likely, considering he is still in his thirties. His decision to marry may also have been influenced by his parents. A reversed Emperor also points to rebellious tendencies. These seem to have been repressed by his need for a stable partnership, and are now surfacing in his affair.

2: The Present is represented by the two of Swords, revealing the inquirer's subjective view of his situation. The card is reversed, suggesting selfishness, and lies. It also denotes some kind of release from his situation, a lessening of pressure is likely. However, it also warns him that he is being rather selfish and tending to think only of himself.

3: Hidden factors are symbolized by Temperance. A Major card here reveals just how important these probably unconscious motives are, Temperance speaks of balance, of a harmony between the spiritual and physical worlds.

Our inquirer seeks to balance opposing forces in his life, and appears to have created a situation where stability, represented by his marriage, opposes mystery and adventure, represented by his secretive and possibly unattainable lover. This conflict has also appeared in his career, but he is on the verge of resolving it there. Temperance provides him with serious food for thought.

4: Negative influences are represented by the three of Wands. This is a very positive and helpful career card and at first sight appears to be somewhat incongruous in this position. However, there are various ways to interpret it. Since our inquirer's inner conflicts are working themselves out in both career and love life, it could be that he has used this love affair as a way of giving his life meaning.

He has been trapped in a job which no longer satisfies him for very long, and has been seeking some kind of release. The other woman represents a challenge. Since she was formerly represented by the High Priestess in our first layout, she also suggests the kind of visionary imagination the inquirer will be able to bring to his new business. This was symbolized by the Queen of Cups, who also indicated that he would be emotionally satisfied by this new venture.

5: Other people's views are symbolized by the Page of Cups. Since the inquirer's wife does not know about his affair, this card represents his lover. Her feelings could be changing towards him. She is certainly emotionally involved with him, but does not seem to be deeply attached as yet.

6: The best course of action is represented by the Moon. Here the inquirer is being gently pushed towards his feminine, intuitive side. His dreams contain important messages, his instincts and feelings are surfacing. All of this can be very disturbing, and hard to handle. Outside help would be a sensible option at this time, for he is unlikely to be able to make much sense of his subconscious without it.

7: The most likely result is represented by Death. Significant major changes are indicated here. Old attitudes and outworn concepts are dying and both the inquirer's inner and outer life will be affected. It will not be easy for him, but it is important to stress that Death holds a promise of rebirth. It is safe to say that, after considerable struggles our inquirer will emerge as a wiser, more self-aware person.

NOTES